ON POINT

Vernice,

I hope you enjoy the book.
I hope they inspire you!

Take care

[signature]

ON POINT

VOICES AND VALUES
OF
THE YOUNG ELECTED OFFICIALS

Jeff L. Thigpen

With a Foreword by

Senator George J. Mitchell

Polar Bear & Company
Solon, Maine

To my wife, Michelle, the best elementary school
principal I know, and our children, Elle and Aiden.

First edition 2012
16 15 14 13 12   1 2 3 4 5 6 7

Polar Bear & Company™
PO Box 311, Solon, Maine 04979 U.S.A.
207.643.2795 www.polarbearandco.org

Library of Congress Control Number: 2012937878
ISBN: 978-1-882190-11-9

Cover design by Ramona du Houx.

Manufactured in the U.S.A. by Thomson-Shore, Inc., an employee-owned
company—certified by the Forest Stewardship Council and a member of the
Green Press Initiative—using soy ink and acid-free, recycled paper of archival
quality, at paper permanence specifications defined by ANSI.NISO standard
Z39.48-992: "The ability of paper to last several hundred years without significant
deterioration under normal use and storage conditions in libraries and archives."

The dogmas of the quiet past are inadequate to the stormy present. The occasion is piled high with difficulty, and we must rise with the occasion. As our case is new, so we must think anew, and act anew. We must disenthrall ourselves, and then we shall save our country.

—ABRAHAM LINCOLN
Second Annual Message to Congress
December 1, 1862

CONTENTS

FOREWORD

Because of the wisdom and foresight of our Founding Fathers, we are fortunate to live in a society that values openness and freedom. From this society each of us receives many benefits. With those benefits comes the responsibility to build a better future. That's why it is incumbent upon us to make certain that young people of today get the chance to go as far  and as high as their talent and willingness will take them.

Young leaders are coming of age in an exciting time of turbulence and change in American life and history. Of course, change has been the norm since the beginning of our Great Republic. Politics in the early years of our country was rough and tumble, and it is no different today.

But American politics has been more partisan and contentious in recent years. In many ways, that reflects the overall mood of our country. We are evenly divided and in conflict over a number of issues that affect our lives, our communities, and the world around us. Whatever your personal or political persuasion, this can be frustrating and disheartening, even for the most optimistic.

I believe that there's no such thing as a conflict that can't be ended. Conflicts are created, conducted, and sustained by human beings. They can be ended by human beings. No matter how divisive, no matter how harmful, our "better angels" can prevail. We can build strong, vibrant communities at home and be partners with others around the world for peace.

As in any worthy endeavor, it is essential that we create an attitude and atmosphere based on the reality that no matter how difficult the problems, they can be solved. Jeff has done an outstanding job of pulling together a number of inspiring stories of young elected officials, who are actively engaged in their local communities on a number of difficult issues and have a hunger to help reshape our society for the better.

On Point gives readers a unique perspective on these leaders, speaking in their own voices. The reader gets to know who they are and what is important to them, personally as well as politically. So much of what I value in public service has come from my own life story and from those friends and colleagues who influenced my personal and political development and growth.

My family has been central to my life. My mother was an immigrant from Lebanon. She came to the United States in 1920, when she was eighteen years old. My father was the orphaned son of immigrants from Ireland. He never knew his parents. My parents had no education. My mother couldn't read or write English. She worked nights in a textile mill. My father was a janitor at a college in our hometown.

But they were part of that generation of Americans that had a very deep commitment to the education of their children. They had, really, an exaggerated notion of the value of education. But their life's goal was to see to it that their children received the education that they never got. In that, they were successful. They had five children, all of whom went on to graduate from college.

Because of their efforts, and because of the openness of American society, I was able to get the education they never had and pursue opportunities I had never imagined. I served as majority leader of the United States Senate and have traveled the world, working with others seeking peace in the Middle East and helping achieve it in Northern Ireland.

But one of my greatest achievements came when I left the U.S. Senate and created the George J. Mitchell scholarship program for Maine students with financial need. It started small, and we now provide a scholarship every year to a graduate from each of the 130 public high schools in the state.

The scholarship program is gratifying to me, because as a young person I was not sure I was going to college. My parents had no money, and my father was not working at the time. I got lots of help from a lot of people. When I meet with students each year, I see in them a lot of where I was at the time, uncertain, insecure, and not sure what they are going to do in life, but full of potential. I not only see the potential, I hear the voices of a new generation of Americans.

I hear in their voices the potential to assure that every American child is entitled to a good education, regardless of background or family wealth. I hear in their voices the obligation to leave for future generations the very basics of healthy human life: clean air, pure water, unpoisoned land, and public policies to honor that obligation. I hear in their voices the commitment that every American is entitled to equal opportunity and equal justice.

The challenges we face as a nation will require responsibility from every American. Every individual in every sector of our society will have to assume a fair share of responsibility to address our nation's ills. The debates will be lively. There will be differences of opinion, but we must move quickly and prudently.

The issues are complicated. It will not be easy. No worthy endeavor is ever easy. But it can be done. I hear it in the voices of those leaders featured in *On Point* as they embark on the eternal struggle to build a more perfect union in the United States of America.

George J. Mitchell
Waterville, Maine
November, 2011

INTRODUCTION

"Hi, [insert: constituent name]!

"That's a nice [insert: dog, cat, flower, car, or shrub]."

[Insert smile: ☺]

"My name is Jeff Thigpen, and I'm running for county commissioner. I'm running because I want the commissioners to be about leadership, not partisanship."

They are fighting like the dickens, and most of us are tired of it.

"Public education is my number-one issue. I believe we need to approve school bonds to renovate outdated facilities and build new ones."

We haven't built or renovated schools in twenty-five years, and we fight with the School Board regularly.

"Secondly, I'm against the food tax for a new baseball stadium."

Everyone's against it.

"And lastly," conventional wisdom says to talk in threes, "I just wanted to meet you, and I'd appreciate your vote!"

It's November 2, 1998. I've been captive to this statement 7,321 times over the past seven months. It has opened many heavy, wooden doors in Greensboro, North Carolina. I've covered several streets on this unusually warm day in the historic Spring Garden neighborhood. Each house brings a new face and a new opportunity to make a connection. All my senses are tingly, finely tuned and focused on the prize, because tomorrow is Election Day.

With each step, my hopes and fears collide within what feels to me like the world's smallest particle accelerator. Fueled by Mountain Dew and Snickers bars, it produces random thoughts circulating through my head and guts at the speed of light, continually smashing into one another as I race through the neighborhood like a marathon runner, tossing soda cans and candy wrappers at appropriate places along the route.

I'm caught in an adrenaline- and sugar-induced rush. I scribble down notes while taking in the smells of freshly mowed grass and grilled something-or-other over charcoals in a nearby backyard. I've been moving door to door, fumbling through dog-eared "walk lists" since 9 a.m. in this small but favorable precinct. It's nearing twilight, and I arrive at my very last door as the sun fades. It's the home of an unaffiliated voter, who casts her ballots like Jesus prayed—religiously. Her name is Minota Jones.

As I walk up to the screen door, I spy a pot of flowers on the front steps. "Nice tulips" is about to roll off my tongue as I hear Minota sliding her slippers toward the door. In the last of the day's light, I notice two young-looking, wondrous eyes, which seem intent on denying her elderly state and frail body. They don't appear to be looking for a politician or a solution to a problem.

Minota's classic Southern accent digs at me on cognitive and intuitive levels from the moment she says hello. There's something about her that is disarming, soothing, and her words activate memories from a familiar place that's been locked away for a while. Thoughts of home emerge immediately. The sight of morning dew and smells of cured ham, fresh black dirt, diesel fuel and axle grease, the comfort of a cool breeze in the shade after cropping tobacco all day, fishing on the bank of the Cape Fear River. I begin to relax a little.

"Young man, would you like to come in?" she asks, after giving me the once-over. She takes my flyer and sets it politely on her coffee table, never giving it a glance. She serves me cookies and tea, and shows me her journal of inspirational quotes accumulated over eighty-eighty years of living. I'm beginning to wonder whether UPS and pizza-delivery men—and perhaps previous candidates for office—have settled into her cushiony couch, never to be heard from again.

Minota has no idea what I'm running for, and I don't think she really cares. Her disinterest in the Guilford County Board of Commissioners could not be greater. She isn't curious about my platform or my bullet points. What she wants to hear is my story. Her invitation and intent gaze gently lead me back to a small hospital in southeastern North Carolina ten months earlier.

* * *

I am holding onto my father's hand and watching his lips closely. His body is still and frail. It bears scars from years of pain management and a series of strokes. Each breath grows gradually weaker and lighter.

I am transported back to the day when my mother, sister, brother, and I almost lost him, twenty-two years earlier in October 1975. He was kicking loose an ear of corn from the harvester when one of the spinning prongs snagged his pants leg and pulled him into the combine. His left leg was destroyed in a matter of seconds, his body jammed into the machine until a passing highway patrolman heard his shouts and turned it off. My father was cut out of the combine with blowtorches and raced to the hospital.

I remember that day as clearly as a five-year-old can. I had been with my mom on that combine in the same field earlier in the day, before my dad took over after his day job at our local ABC store. We pulled into the driveway. Our black-and-tan hunting dog burrowed under the fence, jumped through the passenger door of the pickup truck, and grabbed a steak out of our bag of groceries. I sat in the truck giggling as my mom started yelling and chasing the dog around the yard. Minutes later, still worked up over the dog, she answered the phone. She immediately became motionless and nearly faint. It was the first time I had experienced the overwhelming feeling that something was terribly wrong.

At about the same time, a paramedic nicknamed Curly was asking my barely conscious father if he felt anything.

He responded, "No."

Curly said, "Tommy, we need you to hang on."

My father replied, "Curly, I have to—I have three children to raise."

Against all odds, and by all accounts, Tommy Thigpen cheated death and survived. He spent 318 days in the hospital, enduring multiple surgeries and numerous skin grafts, and recovering from the psychological and emotional trauma.

In a hospital room twenty-two years later, my eyes are acutely focused on my dad's lack of movement, and I have a weird ringing in my ears, probably from the silence. I'm either in complete shock or in some illuminative state of grace. I feel an equal measure of terror and awe as life and death seem to inhabit the same space right in front of me.

Then, as if on cue from central casting, a local clergyman walks in. We lower our heads and pray together. Within minutes, the monotone of the EKG monitor is the only sound in the room.

My family members and I console one another and thank the Indian doctor with the lilting accent and caring bedside manner. A nurse hovers while I gather our belongings and stare into the absence of life. As I pull the last chip out of a bag of Doritos and throw the crumpled bag in the trash, I hear a startling beep, beep, beep.

I look incredulously at the nurse, who explains that it's Pulseless Electrical Activity (PEA), a response after death, when cells are still technically alive. I nod politely but respond with absolute conviction, *Just like my dad—cheated death one last time.*

I sit back down and grab my father's hand once again. At that moment I feel the most important lesson I will ever learn: I'm loved by a force that is more than I am. I don't have to run from it or deny it; that love is just there to be accepted and given to others. I have no idea where, when, or how, but I have a burning desire to go out into the world, find some lost cause, and make a difference.

* * *

I talk with Minota Jones for close to two hours. I share no talking points, no ideology, no parroted rhetoric. We are just two people connecting around our stories. I think of those difficult days after my father's accident.

My dad was the kind of person who used his CB radio to help stranded motorists late at night, and my mom's indomitable spirit earned her two distinctions as "Carolina Mama," in reference to being the world's greatest UNC Basketball fan and to her stint as the "Pender Chick-a-dee" (knockoff of the San Diego Chicken), tumbling around our local middle school gym as the mascot during sports events. I remember how after the accident she was by his side every day, shuttling back and forth checking on three kids and trying to hold things together. The strain and stress of my father's injuries and the mounting bills eventually caught up with her. My mother suffered from blindness for nearly a year.

For a family whose foundation was hard work, self-reliance, and responsibility, we became for a time hopelessly dependent on the good will of others. We discovered that we were not an island, but part of a community with shared values and shared responsibilities. And when the chips were down for us, someone always seemed to drop by with a cake, some collard greens, or boiled peanuts. That's what good neighbors do in civil societies.

People from a spectrum of ages, races, and classes came to help in the ways they could. The local AM radio station, the Lions Club, and others raised money on our behalf to help pay the bills and enable us to stay in our recently built home. Though there was certainly a feeling in our household that events were constantly unfolding beyond our control, we experienced a nucleus of love and support that stabilized us through the painful days.

Powerful moments came to me at ball games and in convenience stores when strangers asked my name. "You're Tommy and Geraldine's boy?" This would lead to inquiries about how my parents were faring. There was always deeper impact beneath the surface; I could see it in their eyes and hear it in their voices. My family name carried an embedded message for those who had experienced pain, loss, and difficulty: You are not alone, and we're all in this together.

In such a short period, we went from being a working-class family moving our way into the middle class to a family in the middle of crisis working to find a way to make ends meet one day at a time. Eventually my mother got a job in the cafeteria of our middle school. Uncle Sam helped us, too, sending Social Security disability checks. The added income made all the difference in the world back then. Today, the monthly Social Security tax deductions I pay are more about paying it forward and being grateful that leadership in government generations ago saw fit to establish a shared investment in our shared future, so our family had a hand up until we got back on our feet.

My father kept his promise to Curly. Together, my parents raised those three kids. My father's sheer endurance and will to live, along with my mom's ability to overcome hardship like a monster truck, are embedded in their children's DNA.

The passion I felt to make a change in the world after my father's death spilled over into an opportunity that came much sooner than I expected. When I returned home to Greensboro, I was approached by a county commissioner and a local activist about running for a seat in a district election for the Board of Commissioners. I pondered it right to the last minute.

On the last day for filing, I walked into my local Board of Elections and presented a $125 check to the clerk. That check and some paperwork launched me on the journey that led to Minota Jones's door on the last day before the general election. The next day, I got Minota's vote—and quite a few others—and was elected the youngest county commissioner in the history of Guilford County. I was twenty-seven years old.

* * *

The path to elected office is anything but easy for those who want to serve. Many candidates think they have all the right moves and words but don't know how to inspire neighbors and win a campaign. And those who end up winning are usually disheartened when they realize that they'll be spending more time politicking and resisting institutional rigor mortis than achieving the goals that inspired them to run. Politics can seem like a never-ending cycle of power plays, backroom deals, and ethical jujitsu working its way out of the state Legislature or the City Hall on the corner of Machiavelli and Constitution Avenues. It can feel like putting together a jigsaw puzzle using the wrong lid as a model and with missing pieces nowhere to be found.

If conflict is a growth industry, then politics should be a Fortune 500 company. No matter what the jurisdiction, tensions tend to rise and fall like the stock market and escalate when particular needs, interests, and passions collide in the pursuit of that "more perfect union" or in opposition to that nearby landfill. Whether it's about stray dogs or energy policy, we just don't agree all the time, and getting from the world we're in to the world as we want it isn't easy.

If you're a politician in the majority, there's the pressure and responsibility that come from knowing that you can make policy with all the intended and/or unintended consequences. In the minority, there's the pressure and responsibility to push one's own agenda, and it comes with a license to undermine your opponent. Regardless of the position you take, you can usually depend on one side or the other to exacerbate any missteps and use any arrows you might give them to take you down.

The Athenians faced such headaches and mulled over similar dilemmas a couple thousand years before anybody stood outside a polling place, greeting voters at the Rec Center. Some challenges have persisted since the dawn of democracy. And some are unique to this moment in history.

The United States is suffering under the worst economic reality since the Great Depression. There's no shortage of people who want work, and long-term unemployment is at its highest in recent memory. The financial services industry that played Russian roulette with our futures was bailed out, while the vast majority of Americans struggle day after day and don't see things getting any better for them.

According to recent polls, nearly 75 percent of Americans believe the country is headed in the wrong direction. Congressional job approval numbers are worse, with nearly 85 percent of Americans expressing disapproval. We are caught up in what feels like a perpetual culture war, ignited and sustained by vehemently partisan politics.

Despite this bleak picture, from an unexpected corner comes hope. Operating largely beneath the national radar, a group of young elected officials is defying the traditional expectation of being the "next" generation of leaders and is offering courageous and creative leadership right now at local and state levels all across the country. America's future national political leaders most likely will be found among these go-getters. Somewhere in a local town hall, a future U.S. president may be sweating over a taxation issue or rezoning decision.

Young people by no means have a monopoly on innovation and ideas, but they tend to be willing to try out new things. And, let's face it, we need lots of new and bold ideas these days. It's time to build some new scaffolding, to make progress on some of our age-old problems—from job creation to education, from national security to building sustainable communities and providing health care for all of our citizens.

We need to grow beyond the hollow arguments about whether government is too big or too small or whether it is by nature the problem or the solution. The truth is, most people just want government to work for our common interests again. At its core, government should be a partnership in our shared future, and our leaders should work for the commonwealth of interests in which we all have a stake, from the school board up to the presidency. America needs to recapture a spirit of civic virtue, with political leaders who serve the people who elected them, not the corporate coffers and special interests that funded their campaigns. It's time for the prosperity of our financial systems to help those who work for it and not just those at the top, if we want to rebuild the country we love. Those values lead us toward an America built to last.

My personal story has taught me that we are strongest when we affirm the worth, dignity, and potential of every individual, even when we disagree, when we join together to help those in need, when opportunity and basic fairness make our abundance accessible to all. I have learned that generosity and compassion will gain us far more security than coercion and domineering self-interest. My story also assures me that, even in the midst of trouble, doubt, and fear, something new is always waiting to be born, to emerge with transforming power.

I have chosen to focus this book on other young leaders who share this perspective, whose leadership is marked by an inclusive and progressive vision. Their compelling stories, like my own, have shaped their work as politicians, as they serve on town and city councils, school boards, county commissions, and state legislatures across this nation.

Such stories can help us to remember where we've been and where we can go. They can impart strength and courage when our principles and values meet the hard-and-fast realities of politics-as-it-is, when our consciousness is torn and in need of a deeper wisdom. They can help us recover from failure and keep us anchored in success, as we seek to serve and respond to the challenges of the 21st century.

I believe deeply in the principles of America, and I love my family and my country. We are going through tough times, but I'm from the Great Melting Pot/We the People school. I don't care if you're a Democrat, Republican, Libertarian, Vegetarian, Liberal, Conservative, Christian, Muslim, Catholic, Atheist, or Agnostic. Whether we like it or not, we are all in this together.

America needs all of us, and it's time we stop hedging and go all in. If you have the opportunity to get involved, to make a difference in the lives of others through service—do it. I hope this book offers you an opportunity to reflect upon your core values, what aligns your head and heart, and what ignites your passion in service to others as we seek to leave our neighborhoods and communities better than we found them.

I spent two years interviewing more than one hundred young elected officials—from Alaska to Florida and Maine to California. I posed four primary questions:

What is your personal history?

What inspired you to run for public office?

What have you learned in campaigns and as an elected leader?

What advice would you give to other young people considering a run for elected office?

All of these inspiring young leaders qualify for inclusion in this volume. I chose a sampling that highlights a diversity and balance of gender, geography, ethnicity, and position.

Anton Gunn always wanted to be a leader, as he was as a football player for the University of South Carolina and community organizer after graduation. He entered politics after his brother Cherone was killed aboard the *USS Cole* during the al-Qaeda attack in October 2000. He served in the South Carolina House of Representatives.

Faith Winter had her first child while in office. She's breaking down barriers for women and advocating for the needs of young people and families. When she took her seat on the Westminster City Council, she was the youngest elected woman in Colorado.

Alex Cornell du Houx is a Marine Corps veteran who served in Iraq. There he learned the realities of war and the illusions of over-dependence on oil. In the Maine House of Representatives, he advocates for veterans' benefits, health care, and renewable energy.

Alicia T. Morgan didn't wait for someone to tell her she was old enough to act. Involved as a teenager with the NAACP and now serving one of Georgia's most conservative districts in the state House of Representatives, she demonstrates the power that comes when young people have the courage to organize and take tough stands in face of adversity.

Compassion for his patients and concern about our broken health-care system led Dr. Matt Heinz to run for the Arizona Legislature after a long night in Tucson's ER. He believes that health care is a state- and national-security issue in which government has a role. He is a persistent advocate for preventive medicine and other life-giving measures for his constituents.

Dominic Frongillo serves on the Town Council of his hometown of Caroline in upstate New York. Focused on climate change and its devastating effects, he attended the UN climate negotiations in Bali, Copenhagen, and Cancun. As part of Lighten Up Caroline, he went door to door with a hundred other volunteers to deliver 1,400 energy-efficient light bulbs across fifty-five square miles in three hours.

The eldest of fourteen children, Rashida Tlaib is Arab American and the first Muslim elected to the Michigan state Legislature, where she represents southwest Detroit. Committed to improving neighborhoods, she understands the "power of convening" to reach across traditional divisions to bring change.

Rodney Glassman was a Jewish boy in a Mormon Boy Scout troop, who attended a Catholic high school. By age thirty-two, he had earned five advanced degrees. He ran against John McCain for the U.S. Senate in Arizona in 2010. Accepting no contributions over $20, he was outspent 32 to 1 and lost the election but won points on health care in their televised debate. He served as vice-mayor of Tucson.

The daughter of Chinese immigrants, Janet Chin served with the Army National Guard in Haiti, where she cultivated a love for youth work. She is president of the Garvey School District in California, whose students speak eight primary languages. During her tenure, the district has received several awards for distinguished achievement.

Rev. Dr. Simeon Queen grew up in the heart of the Christian mega-church movement and evangelical movement in Texas. As a person of faith and elected official, Simeon seeks to live a life of passion and principle as he serves on the Prairie View City Council and as pastor of Homeless Services at St. John's United Methodist Church in Houston, Texas.

Marisol Cruz came to the United States in the hands of "coyotes," smugglers that helped her family cross from Mexico when she was a child. Her California community is 98 percent Latino, and the local school system's decision to take away classes in Spanish and immersion programs that help children learn English spurred her into politics. She campaigned for the Lennox School Board with her two young sons in tow.

As a high school student, Sara Humm qualified by three days for the minimum age of eighteen to run for office. In 2007 she was the youngest elected official in America. She served on the City Commission in her hometown of Ottawa, Kansas.

Kevin Killer is a U.S. citizen, a South Dakota citizen, and a tribal citizen in the third most impoverished community in the United States. Against overwhelming odds, he fights for the basic needs of his people and for rural empowerment.

In middle and high school, Shane Cohn carried copies of the Bible and the U.S. Constitution, finding inspiration in both. He left the Army when he realized that its Don't Ask Don't Tell policy didn't allow him to live honestly. He survived smear tactics during his campaign to win a seat as an alderman in St. Louis, Missouri.

Kyrsten Sinema is on the front lines of change in Arizona. Obsessed as a child with learning about the civil rights movement and confronting racism, she took on Arizona's controversial immigration policy in the state Legislature.

Airick Leonard West shows us the value of a loving family. His life story is an example of hardship and survival that have fueled his endurance, stubbornness, and fierce advocacy for the children in the Kansas City school system.

These young leaders represent many others who serve with integrity, compassion, and vision. The Young Elected Officials (YEO) Network offers support for these leaders, reflecting the values of freedom, fairness, and opportunity. Together they are a sign of hope in troubled times. It would serve us well to pay attention to their stories.

With new energy and new ideas, there is great promise in the nature of our American republic to change and once again respond to the will of its people. A new generation of problem solvers has the unique ability and opportunity to become reformers of the systems that we need in order to build ever-increasing opportunities for all to help out and prosper.

Young leaders represent the emergence of the largest generational shift in our nation's history. They are dynamic, diverse, and are having impacts on American society that will only increase with time in every sector, social, political, economic, civic, and religious. Young leaders have the capacity and they will bear an increasing responsibility to help America rouse itself from the robotic trance of complacency, seek a higher level of consciousness, capture our hearts and minds, and embody a more engaged citizenship in the 21st century.

If you are an increasingly seasoned leader like me, you'll gain an understanding of how these young leaders think and see the world around them. If you are a young reader and leader, I know my children will look toward you for leadership and guidance in the years to come. And if for that reason alone, I pledge my full support in creating a newer world, a newer America.

I never really saw myself as an elected official until it was crystallized by my brother's death. Cherone was aboard the *USS Cole* in October 2000 when al-Qaeda attacked the ship. He and the sixteen others who died that day died defending a country we love. My brother gave the ultimate sacrifice, and it helped me realize the true meaning of public service.

Anton J. Gunn
South Carolina House of Representatives

History

I GREW UP THE OLDEST OF four brothers. Mom was a public school teacher, and Dad was in the Navy for twenty-two years. From an early age, around fourteen or fifteen, I knew I wanted to be a leader. Whether as captain of the football team or organizing kids at my school to put on a concert against violence, I just wanted to lead. I remember in the ninth grade I wanted to be the first African American governor of the state of Virginia. But then a year later Doug Wilder got elected, so I lost my chance.

In college I played football at the University of South Carolina, started a student-athlete advocacy organization there, and served as a representative to the Southeastern Conference on student-athlete issues. When I graduated, I started doing work as a community organizer, knocking on doors and working in communities and organizing people around issues. I guess being an elected leader was always in the back of my mind, although I never really saw myself as an elected official until it was crystallized by my brother's death.

My brother Cherone was aboard the *USS Cole* in October 2000, when al-Qaeda attacked the ship. I can still recall all the details. It was a Thursday morning, and I was at work. I got a call from my mother, who told me she had received a call from the Navy stating that there had been an explosion aboard my brother's ship.

When I couldn't get enough information via the Internet and phone, I decided to go to my local bank, which was close by and had CNN playing on the television. I learned that thirteen people on the ship were missing and four were confirmed dead. I had been standing in the bank for about an hour when my phone rang. It was my dad. I could hear nothing but his screams and cries through the phone as he said, "They killed my son!"

I collapsed right there in the lobby of the bank. What was going through my mind was, *Why?* I mean, we were at peace. This was before 9/11. This was before most people in America knew who Osama bin Laden or al-Qaeda were, so why would someone kill my brother?

Cherone was one of the nicest people anyone could meet. He never met a stranger. We used to call him the "love child," because he was born on Valentine's Day in 1978.

I have so many fond memories of him. The thing that I am struggling the most with now is that when Cherone and I were growing up, we used to joke about who was going to be the best uncle to the other's children—that would be the one who would spoil them the most. I now have a young daughter named Ashley. What I miss the most is that Ashley will grow up never knowing who her Uncle Cherone was. She won't get to feel his embrace and have him play games with her in the yard or buy her nice things and say, "This is from your Uncle Cherone. Don't tell your dad I bought it for you." I'm sad that my daughter won't get to experience that.

The last conversation Cherone and I had was over email. He used to send me all kinds of crazy jokes. But on that occasion, he sent a personal email. He said that he had seen lots of interesting places and that he hadn't realized that the world was that big and beautiful. He said, "I love you, and I'll talk with you in a little while." That was the last I heard from him.

The thing I wish I could tell him is that his legacy in life lives through us every single day. I wish I could hold him and touch him now. I wish I could be with him somehow. I wish I could tell him that I know he is in a better place, and I know he is smiling down on us, and that I love him.

Cherone and the sixteen others who died that day died defending a country we love. They died for us. I remember kneeling at his casket during his funeral, telling him that I loved him and was going to miss him, and clutching the flag from his casket to my chest after the service—the last physical piece I have of him.

I did a lot of speaking out after the tragedy—on *Good Morning America*, CNN, *CBS Evening News*—about the personal consequences of terrorism, as well as the implications and security issues affecting all Americans. When thinking and talking about my brother, I realized that most elected leaders just talk about public service. My brother gave the ultimate sacrifice, and it helped me realize the true meaning of public service. I credit Cherone with getting me on the road to politics.

Politics

I SAW TOO MANY PEOPLE IN politics who I thought were not authentic, not committed, and not accountable. And as a result, our communities were suffering, just as my family and the country were suffering from the terrorist attack. I realized that if this is the leadership we have at the highest levels of our country, then we are in a bad spot. The only way we were going to be better was to have better leaders. Instead of me looking for someone else to be a leader, I asked myself, why don't I just become one?

In 2004 I had moved to the other side of Columbia, South Carolina, where my wife had grown up, because she wanted to live closer to her parents and be in a good place to raise our children. This part of the city is very white and upper-middle class. At the time, I said, "There goes my political career," because I believed I had moved into a community in which I could never get elected.

But I knew a lot about community issues and about statewide policy issues, and I also knew how to connect the dots among communities with a regional perspective. The political situation in the state bothered me, and I decided that I didn't care if I lost; I just needed to talk about what I wanted to talk about.

I ran for the state Legislature in 2006. I ran against a twelve-year incumbent Republican, who had served eight years on the school board before he was in the state Legislature, so he had twenty years of name recognition and experience of serving people in that district. On election night, the Democratic Party announced that I had won, and everyone was celebrating. Then the absentee ballots came in. I lost by 298 votes.

I ran in the same district in 2008. When I announced that I was running, the incumbent announced that he was going to retire and not seek reelection. I restructured my whole organization.

In 2006 I had raised $67,000 and spent $70,000. In 2008 I raised $126,000 and spent $130,000. In the second campaign I had a lot more knowledge about things, because I had worked on Obama's campaign for year. The two people on my core staff cut their teeth on the 2008 primary with the Obama and Bill Richardson campaigns.

One of the co-chairs of my steering committee was actually a precinct leader for my Republican opponent in 2006. He had watched me and was convinced that I was smart and had a bright future. After my former opponent retired, this guy called me immediately. I went over to his house, and he gave me a $250 check. He invited all his friends over to meet me, and he helped me with nonstop encouraging and recruiting Republicans and others to help me win. He saw me as a breath of fresh air, as the kind of guy who would walk down the aisle on both sides and work with Republicans and Democrats to get stuff done.

Campaigning

THE AVERAGE HOUSE DISTRICT IN SOUTH CAROLINA contains about 33,000 people. My district, which is the fastest growing in the state, is about three times as large. My voters are very educated: 98 percent are high school graduates, 63 percent have college degrees, and 36 percent have a masters, law, or PhD degree. I had to canvass door to door and launch a sophisticated direct-mail effort. I also did AM and FM radio sports, maintained a website and email list. And I did a lot of barbecues and fish fries.

In my district, which is largely suburban, there are lots of single-family homes and cul-de-sacs, some gated communities. It is very spread out, and a lot of people don't even know their neighbors, much less the people who are running for office. I had to knock on doors in a lot of these communities to have a chance to win.

In 2006 I went into a subdivision where it was obvious that the only people that came into it were either residents or UPS or FedEx guys coming in to deliver packages. I pulled up in a cul-de-sac and started knocking on doors. I knocked on the door of one house, and no one was home; second house, no one was home. At the third house, I saw a woman in a van backing out of her driveway.

I knocked at two more houses, and then I went back to the house where I had seen the van leaving. I thought maybe the woman's husband was home. I rang the doorbell and heard a small dog inside yapping really loudly. While I was standing on the porch, marking on my clipboard that no one was home, the van that I saw back out of the driveway came speeding up the road and to a screeching halt. The woman jumped out and pulled a gun on me.

I learned later that she had left her two young children, both under the age of ten, in the house while she made a quick run to the store. She had seen my car sitting near her house and realized that she had never seen that car in her neighborhood before. Then she saw me at a vacant house across the street. By the time I got to her house, with the dog yapping, one of her children had called her on the phone and said, "Mommy, there is a man on our porch at our house."

She had spun around and come back, because she thought someone was trying to break into her house and do something to her children. To compound the situation, her husband, who was in the military, had just been called away to Iraq. So she was scared to death that something bad was happening.

When she pulled the gun on me, I froze. But I stayed on message: "Hello ma'am, my name is Anton Gunn and I'm running for the state House of Representatives because I believe we need new leadership, and I'm out in the community today talking to neighbors about my campaign." I handed her a flyer; she looked at it and saw that the picture was of me, then she put the gun down. She apologized profusely for pulling the gun.

I was pretty scared. I gave her voter registration forms and went to my car, got in, and drove straight home. I couldn't knock on doors for a month afterwards because I was so paranoid and afraid to go into those communities. But I was proud that I had stayed on message, which demonstrated to me that I was committed.

Part of my district is in an adjoining county, which is more rural. Eighty-two percent of the registered voters there are white, and they vote much more conservatively than the other parts of my district. If

Mickey Mouse were on the ballot as a Republican, he'd beat Jesus if he were on the ballot as a Democrat.

I knew one Democrat in this district, who invited all her friends over to meet me one Wednesday night. We had a few snacks, and then she introduced me to the fourteen neighbors who had showed up. I'm a public school supporter, who is in favor of raising the state's cigarette tax to provide more resources for health care. Those were major points in my stump speech. I said that I support not big government but good government for the people.

I didn't know anything about these fourteen people, except that they lived on Cindy's street. It turns out they were all parents whose children were being home-schooled or educated in private schools. In South Carolina, we have proposed legislation that would take money from public schools and give it to parents that either home-school or have their children educated in private schools, through vouchers or tax credits. I am totally opposed to that.

The people in the room were also cigarette smokers—not just one or two, but five of the fourteen. None of them had ever voted for a Democrat, and some had refused to vote for the incumbent Republican, because they consider themselves more Libertarian than Republican.

So I'm sitting there talking about supporting public education and raising cigarette taxes in a room full of Libertarian-Republican chain smokers who want us to give public money to private schools. I stayed there probably four and a half hours with those people. And at the end of the day, they all voted for me.

In that part of the county, one day I pulled up to the house of a woman who had one of my yard signs displayed beside one of John McCain's. She was going to vote for John McCain because she votes Republican, but she also believed in me.

I was up by about two hundred votes when the precinct polls closed, but I was cautious because I knew what could happen with absentee ballots, which didn't get counted until about 11:30 that night. I received almost twice as many absentee votes as my opponent, increasing my margin significantly. I won with about 54 percent of the vote and became the first African American to represent my district.

Advice

We don't have a lot of young legislators in South Carolina. Those we do have aren't in leadership positions. Most legislators are fifty-plus and in the Republican Party.

I have learned that partisanship is not a bad thing; you can believe in your core principles and act out of them from the standpoint of a political party. But blind partisanship is definitely a bad thing. When you believe in the party to the extent that you ignore other good ideas because they come from someone in a different party, that is awful and stupid. We have so much blind partisanship in our state Legislature that is not productive.

The second thing I've learned is this is hard. Being a good elected official is very different from being a good candidate. What you get criticized for more than anything else is not showing up for the barbecue or the church picnic, or not hanging out in the grocery store. I don't mind showing up at events and shaking hands, but if you want me to do a good job, sometimes I need to research policy or go to a state conference.

Doing what the job requires may not be what people get excited about you doing, but you need to follow the practices and policies that move the state forward to make people's lives better. I try to do this both as a legislator and in my work as president of Top Gunn Associates, my consulting firm. We work hand in hand with clients to develop and implement strategies for leadership development, management, advocacy, empowerment, and education.

You have to believe you can be a transformative leader in the 21st century. Being young and getting involved early means you can leave a legacy that lasts long beyond your life. But in order to be effective, you have to master some essentials. I call it "the audacity of leadership."

1. Have a vision for your community and see the big picture of what you are trying to accomplish.
2. Be committed enough to see it through to the end.
3. Be authentic with yourself and others. If you have flaws, let folks know you are flawed. No one is perfect. Be true to yourself, so people can see the true leader you are.
4. Listen to people you are trying to help. If you are not willing to listen to the people you want to serve, then don't run.

5. Be selfless. Remember this is not about you. You are doing this to serve honorably and admirably.

6. Have an attitude of greatness. You have to believe you are the best candidate for office. You may not be the smartest, but you have to believe you are the best.

7. Be willing to talk to anyone. That is the lesson of Cindy's house party. You have to be willing gain people's respect, even if they oppose you. Second, if you have a compelling vision and argument, then don't be afraid to go into "the belly of the beast." There are two things you can come out with. First, you will have earned their respect for your willingness to go to see them, and second you may come out with their vote.

8. Surround yourself with those from whom you can learn, and build a leadership team of those who are the best. If you want to be a great elected official, find someone on whom you can model yourself.

9. Don't wait for permission to lead.

Throughout the race, I was told that I was too young, that I didn't have enough experience. But for many voters, especially young families, my age was seen as a strength. During the campaign, I tried to emphasize my new ideas, my passion, my energy, and the positive aspects of being young. During a community event, one of my opponents actually told me he had socks older than I am. I told him he needed a new pair of socks.

Faith Winter
City Council, Westminster, Colorado

History

MY MOTHER WAS A DEMOCRAT AND my father a Republican, and I think it's the greatest thing in the world that can happen for you. Most kids grow up adopting their parents' views, but I was steeped in political conversations and opinions from both sides, and I had to choose. At an early age, I decided the Democrats were for me. When I was in second grade, I campaigned very hard for Dukakis in our school's mock election for president, and I was devastated when he didn't win.

When I was growing up, the idea of offering public service as an adult was obvious to me. My parents were always doing something to help someone make something better. In addition to school-related activities with my mom, I went to the soup kitchen every month with my father, who was a nurse. I grew up believing that I could do anything I wanted to and that I had an obligation to make the world a better place.

But the concept of running for public office was not as clear. I didn't really start thinking about it until I went to a Women's Legislative Breakfast in 2003 with about three hundred other women, who came together to learn about legislation impacting women. I was working for an environmental organization at the time.

I had a conversation that morning with Joan Fitzgerald, who was the first female state Senate president in Colorado. She was the first person to help me believe I could run for public office, and she encouraged me to do it. I had asked her how she managed to be so effective, and she said she was effective when she got to work with smart people. Then she looked at me and told me I should run. She helped me realize that my service could go beyond organizing and that instead of just asking the decision makers for help, I could be one of those decision makers.

I was around politics my whole life, and I really wanted to be a public servant, but I always thought I'd be behind the scenes. I think most women don't see themselves in a public role. A Pew Research Center study done in 2009 showed that three out of four children thought that it is illegal for a woman to be president of the United States—the year after the very public efforts of Hillary Clinton and Sarah Palin.

Given the absence of a woman president, children will make up their own minds as to why that is. With only 17 percent of Congress like me, it's hard for me to identify and to find mentors who have paved the way. It's really hard to be what you can't see.

Around the time of the legislative breakfast, I encountered the White House Project, which recruits and trains women for public office. I liked the motto on their T-shirts: GO VOTE, GO RUN, GO LEAD. I needed a new job, and they needed a new organizer. So I became the National Field Director. I traveled around the country and spent a lot of time talking with women who were already leaders of organizations such as PTAs, Chambers of Commerce, and nonprofits, encouraging them to consider using their leadership skills as elected officials.

About half the women we train are younger than thirty-five. When you get young women in a room, the first question they ask is, "Can I do this and have a family, too?" I think that is one of the biggest barriers to getting more young women in office. Most women in public office are retired from other work, or on their second careers, with their children grown and out of the house.

We work to break down the barriers for young women. We can't tell you it will be easy to be a mother in office, or to be married in office, but we can provide examples of women for whom it has worked. We organize panels of young women, women of color, and women who are working moms. They tell us how they are able to strike a successful balance between family and public service. And they also help to answer the second question that most women ask, "Can I be elected and keep my integrity?"—sharing stories of how they have.

Campaigning

I RAN FOR THE CITY COUNCIL of Westminster, with a population of a hundred thousand people, when I was 27. I kicked off my campaign in May at my birthday party, and I asked supporters to donate twenty-seven dollars to it. Throughout the campaign, I raised $28,000, out-fundraising my opponents six to one by asking every single person I've ever met for a donation.

From the launch of my campaign on, I simply worked harder than everyone else in the race. I won because I knocked on eleven thousand doors between June and November. I was working with the White House Project 7:00 to 4:00 every day and knocking on doors 5:00 to 8:00, and I made fundraising calls during my lunch hour.

It was important to me to keep my full-time job. I couldn't afford to take nine months off to run a campaign. But I was also encouraging and training women across the country—single mothers, women making minimum wage, and survivors of domestic violence who were becoming financially independent—and I wanted to show them that it's possible to run for office and have a job.

It was a lot of work and discouraging at times. At one door, a middle-aged woman answered and listened to my whole spiel: "Hi, I'm Faith Winter, and I'm running for City Council . . ." She said, "Well, that's great, but I honestly think a woman's place is in the home, and I will not be voting for you."

It didn't surprise me, because I knew that view was out there. But it did make me sad for her, because clearly her place has been in the home, consistent with the values she has. I somewhat respect that, but just to know that she will probably never realize her potential for leadership or show the world everything she has to offer is very sad. For me it was one less vote, but for her it was her life.

At another door, a woman told me, "I'll keep this information, but my husband decides who we vote for." Such encounters were very painful, because you want to empower people and get them excited about your candidacy. But you're not out there to change or infringe. I was never going to get those votes, no matter what I said. But as an organizer who trains women to run for office and teaches them about leadership, it was hard for me not to have that conversation.

One of my major issues was the quality of life for our children. At one home I met two kids who loved Little League, but their mother couldn't afford to pay for them to play. I began talking about making after-school programs more accessible.

Throughout the race, I was told that I was too young, that I didn't have enough experience. But for many voters, especially young families, my age was seen as a strength. The average age in Westminster is thirty-five, and I was a voice for that demographic. During the campaign, I tried to emphasize my new ideas, my passion, my energy, and the positive aspects of being young. During a community event, one of my opponents actually told me he had socks older than I am. I told him he needed a new pair of socks.

Three of our City Council's six at-large seats were at stake in that election. I came in second, becoming the youngest elected woman in the state of Colorado. On the night that we were sworn in, I publicly presented my opponent, who also won, with a new pair of socks—"for a new era on City Council." He loved that, and now he's one of my best mentors.

Politics

THE SKILLS IT TAKES TO RUN a good campaign and to govern are totally different. The City Council experience was not what I expected. I had been involved in the state legislative process and expected it to be similar. At the state level, you hold caucus meetings and introduce legislation. But at the local level, with such a small body, the culture of how you make decisions depends on only seven people: the Council members and the mayor. It is much more of a team effort, and deciding how to operate within that team is very important.

In the first year, I barely knew what I was doing. Some of my colleagues were very unsure of me. It took a full year of planning and budgeting and building relationships to really understand the process and how it works, not only at the city level but with the other members of the Council. The subsequent years have been a lot better, and I feel that I have gotten a lot accomplished.

Like many other cities, Westminster has been hit hard with home foreclosures. We couldn't control the banks or the financial markets, but we wanted to help people who are hurting. If they receive financial counseling, up to 70 percent of families who would otherwise lose their homes stay in them. The problem was how to get the information to them. Most of them are struggling and working hard and aren't the type of people who are likely to show up at a public forum.

I proposed that we include information about available resources, including a foreclosure hotline set up through United Way, in the warning letters that the city sends to people who are about to have their water shut off because their bills are overdue. These families are likely to owe on other services as well and to be in jeopardy of foreclosure. We realize that many are getting help, because the city has been shutting off 60 percent less water since we've included our notices. This has been an easy and free way to spread the word, and we've also saved the city lots of money by not having to shut off and turn back on as many water taps.

I'm also proud of my sustainability accomplishments. We just installed four solar panels on three of our city facilities, we are working on rewriting our solid waste code, and we're continuing to look at how we can make our city more "green."

When I talked about making after-school programs more accessible during the campaign, I got some pushback from other candidates, who felt that this should be a concern of the schools and recreation centers but not the City per se. Now I'm the City Council's advisor to the Youth Advisory Panel, and I've increased access to our youth scholarship program. We hold fundraisers to provide scholarships for athletic programs. The two children I met who love Little League are now beneficiaries of those scholarships, and it has made a concrete difference in their lives.

Advice

SHOW UP. I'VE SHOWN UP AND proven that I'm a doer and not a schmoozer, and so I got a lot of donors and volunteers for my campaign. When I said I would door-knock, I door-knocked. When I said I would phone-bank, I phone-banked. Young people can rise to the top very quickly in the political world, as long as you do what you say you're going do. You'll find that you can make many connections very quickly.

Our security organizations are taking very seriously the issues of energy independence, national security, and climate change, which is changing the debate and raising awareness about how our dependence on oil poses a threat to our economy and our security. This should not be a partisan issue. When the Obama administration hosted one of our events, we held a White House press conference on energy and national security with former Secretary of the Navy and Republican U.S. Senator John Warner. My work with the Truman National Security Project included focusing on educating members of Congress and other elected officials on why to take this issue just as seriously as our military is.

Alex Cornell du Houx
Maine House of Representatives

History

I GREW UP IN SOLON, MAINE, population 940. The town is in an extremely beautiful part of the country, and I'm glad I grew up there. But unfortunately Somerset County is one of the most economically challenged areas of the state. The major employer closed its factory years ago.

Like many in the area, my family was on Food Stamps for a while, until my parents worked their way off them. Many of the kids I grew up with didn't imagine themselves going to college, especially not to a private school like Bowdoin, where I graduated with a degree in government and legal studies. Growing up in Solon gave me perspective on many things, helping me to have a better understanding of the economic and social environments that shape different parts of the state, and how legislation impacts them. Community service was an important part of my high school experience.

The idea of serving my country has always interested me. When a military recruiter called, there really wasn't any recruiting, because I wanted to serve. I chose the Marines because I knew that if I had to go into combat, I'd want to be with those who are the best trained. I enlisted as I finished high school, just as I received word that I had been accepted at Bowdoin. It seemed a natural fit, and the Marine Corps base was just three miles from the college in Brunswick.

I was studying the politics of the Middle East in 2006, when I was called to serve in Iraq; I returned over a year later to the same course. Personally, I did not agree with the Iraq war, but it was my duty and honor to go there with my fellow Marines and serve my country. It is my duty to carry out all lawful orders of my commander-in-chief to the fullest extent, regardless of my personal or political opinions.

I learned at a drill weekend that I was going to Iraq, but I purposely did not tell many people, because I didn't want to create a stir on campus. I tried to finish my classes up to midterms and close them out as best I could. It's amazing all the little things you have to think about when you have to leave suddenly and disappear for a year—from my cell phone bill, to deferring my student loans.

As president of the Maine College Democrats, I had worked to increase the number of Democratic organizations on Maine campuses from about three to twenty-three. We organized the largest Student Democrat convention in Maine history, with speakers including Al Franken and Governor John Baldacci, Congressmen Mike Michaud and Tom Allen.

My deployment attracted a lot of media attention. The vice-chair of the Maine Republican Party was quoted in the local paper essentially saying that I would support the insurgents because I belonged to the College Democrats and other progressive groups. He called me "unquestionably un-American." His comments received national attention, and NBC News covered my deployment.

U.S. forces had gone through Fallujah just before I arrived, so the general population did not necessarily trust us. I was a 0351 assault man, which means that my primary job was to work with the infantry to patrol the streets and provide support with explosives and rockets. I blew open the doors, safes, removed trees and other obstacles, but rarely used rockets, because of the risk of collateral damage.

I remember coming across these kids who would ask for water. I would have expected them to ask for candy, and it illustrated to me how debilitated Iraq was, that this country couldn't even provide drinking water to its children. Sadly, most times we couldn't give them water, because we couldn't even carry enough for ourselves. They were a sad symbol to me of the dynamic and vast inequalities between our two countries, and of what we were capable of doing and hadn't yet done.

We would regularly come across lines of cars, trucks, and tractors that were bumper to bumper in 100 degree heat. The people were waiting for gasoline and diesel, and they would literally wait all day. Because of curfews, we had to break up these lines after dark. People would riot against us and risk their lives, because they were so desperate for fuel. It seemed a great irony to me that this oil country was so disabled and destitute because of its dependence upon a single source of energy. Likewise it highlighted how dependent we are on this same fuel. We are basically stuck in a line to oil-rich countries, who don't necessarily have our best interests in mind.

When you are in a foreign country at war, you are on alert 24/7. When I came home, I began to realize the extent to which I was conditioned to observe every little thing. In class I took note of which students were zoning out, the color pen each was using, when they took notes, which students the professor was making eye contact with. All of these little details came to life in a way they never had before. I would walk into a room and immediately scan it, as I had been doing instinctively for a year.

I saw an orange Frisbee at dusk and immediately thought it was a tracer round, and I avoided potholes in Maine roads, because holes in Iraqi roads usually indicated that IEDs (improvised explosive devices) had been planted there. I knew that Maine does not have IEDs, but instinctively I wanted to move away. But after a while you adjust to life here, and a pothole is just an annoying pothole.

Politics

COMMUNITY SERVICE ALLOWED ME TO REALIZE early on that you can fix one instance of a requirement, but to solve the long-term issue you need to change policy. Increasingly this meant going into politics. Helping to build houses for the underserved while serving on the board of Habitat for Humanity, for example, made this very clear. You need to build that vital house, but long-term legislative policy can address the root problems in education, jobs, and economic development. I became even more engaged in politics when I learned, about the lack of services for veterans, many of whom are homeless. The original GI Bill only really paid for my books and meals at college, because it was so outdated. The issues of PTSD (post-traumatic stress disorder) and TBI (traumatic brain injury) were not being addressed adequately. I know a veteran who literally drank away $10,000 because he didn't get the help he needed.

Veterans' services for the most part hadn't been updated to reflect the wars in Iraq and Afghanistan, and we did not do a good job of taking care of those who came home. I started working with other veterans and organizations like the Truman National Security Project, who are working for veterans' benefits and education, including the 21st Century GI Bill. We're seeing a generational shift; when people see veterans' license plates now, they do not automatically think of older veterans.

I was fortunate to be invited to the White House for President Obama's signing of the largest expansion of veterans' funding in the history of the United States. One would think that given the strong support progressives have shown the military—and through a strong, smart, and principled foreign policy—more people would support Democrats. On the other side, many conservatives in power were incompetent regarding Iraq and did not provide our service members with the right equipment. They did not provide the right health care; many veterans suffered from PTSD, TBI, and inadequate treatment, as seen at Walter Reed Army Medical Center. These conservatives did not support the 21st Century GI Bill. And they did not support certain pay raises for the military. Obama was successful in taking out Bin Laden and was a strong and balanced leader in Libya. But the reality is that polling shows conservatives are still more trusted on military issues.

I work with the Truman National Security Project, where in each state we recruit train and position future leaders, elected officials, their staff, nonprofits and other organizations involved in national security issues. I was hired by Truman to run a national campaign called Operation Free, which is a coalition of national security organizations and veterans who have come together on this issue of climate change and our dependence on oil. We have organized with veterans, to help educate lawmakers and the public on this issue, as many are not aware the DOD is reducing their carbon pollution by 25 percent by 2025. And the Navy is launching the Great Green Fleet with hybrid destroyers in 2016. For our efforts we won the best public affairs award of 2010.

We also give trainings on how to work and relate with the military. One member of Congress at a destroyer launching kept calling Marines "soldiers." Every time he did, I could see by the Marines' expression they did not appreciate the mistake, as Marines earned the distinction of being called Marines. You can't make that kind of mistake if you want to have credibility with the military; it shows that you don't understand and you don't care about them. During Military 101 trainings, we talk about how the military has both progressive and conservative values, yet most people don't realize that a lot of the military's values are progressive. For example, "leave no one behind." And officers eat last—so you take care of those you lead and help the less fortunate.

Community service, military service, and public service all have the same overall goal, which is to improve the community. I've had the opportunity to combine the three and am humbled by the support I've received in each to succeed.

Campaigning

DURING MY LAST SEMESTER IN COLLEGE, I was recruited by the House Democratic Campaign Committee to run for the Brunswick seat, District 66, in the Maine House of Representatives in 2008. And I ended up in a three-way race with a Republican and a candidate from the Green Party, where I won by 12 percent. In 2010 I was reelected in another three-way race by 192 votes. This time the Green and the Republican worked very hard for a year to defeat me in one of the most expensive House races in Maine, and each voter in my district got about twenty-five pieces of mail. Because the Green candidate split the vote, I needed to reach beyond the votes I had received last time, and I'm grateful for support both from strong Democrats and Republicans and the Independents who allowed me to keep working for the people of Brunswick and Maine.

I used Facebook and other social networking sites in the campaign, but they were not as significant as door knocking, TV, and direct mail. Intergenerational ties and listening to people at the doors were very important. I would not have been elected without the relationships I developed with current officials and supporters in the process, and I learned a great deal from them. Also, being engaged in community projects is vitally important. I learned so much from serving on the board of Habitat for Humanity, coaching soccer and lacrosse, and as chair of the Mitchell Scholarship Alumni Council.

There is always a tremendous learning curve in the Legislature, as I get engaged in so many issues, because I have to be educated enough to make a solid decision when it comes time to vote. I serve on the Energy Utilities and Technology Committee, where we work on everything from energy, telecom, and water, to new technology. I also served on the Legal and Veterans' Affairs Committee, which deals with everything from veterans' issues, ethics and elections, to gambling, alcohol, and tenants' rights.

I'm also very involved with health-care issues—which include physical education, nutrition, transition to paperless records, and improving education—as well as the composites industry, offshore wind, expanding broadband and Internet services, ways of stimulating the economy in a largely rural state.

I'm particularly passionate about the issue of renewable energy and energy independence, observing firsthand those long lines of Iraqis waiting for gasoline and diesel. The United States spends about one billion dollars overseas for oil every day. The military's Quadrennial Defense Report put climate change as a serious national security issue, and the CIA has opened a center on climate change. The Marines are using flexible solar panels in combat; the Army will have one of the largest electric vehicle fleets in the world, while the Air Force aims to be at 50 percent utilization of biofuel by 2016.

Our security organizations are taking very seriously the issues of energy independence, national security, and climate change, which is changing the debate and raising awareness about how our dependence on oil poses a threat to our economy and our security. This should not be a partisan issue. When the Obama administration hosted one of our events, we held a White House press conference on energy and national security with former Secretary of the Navy and Republican U.S. Senator

John Warner. My work with the Truman National Security Project included focusing on educating members of Congress and other elected officials on why to take this issue just as seriously as our military is. We've spent millions of dollars on TV ads and sponsored three national bus tours. I went from Missoula, Montana, to Brunswick, Maine, talking about this issue and built a network of hundreds of veterans, including many admirals and generals who travel with us across the nation. You can find the details at www.operationfree.net.

My district faced the closure of the military base in Brunswick. We are working hard to replace the jobs and turn it into an opportunity. Now called Brunswick Landing, it has tremendous potential in the areas of renewable energy and the composites, as Maine is a world leader in both emerging industries. There is the equivalent of forty nuclear power plants worth of wind power off one section of Maine's coast. We have the first composite bridge in the nation, which lasts longer and is lighter and cheaper. I've worked on successful legislation with the legislative delegation to bring the University of Maine's and Southern Maine Community College's advanced composite program to Brunswick Landing, providing the basis for building windmills, and we are already creating high-paying, quality jobs. We can never replace the culture of service the military community brought to Brunswick, but we can replace the jobs to strengthen Brunswick and Maine.

Campaigning is not just for elections; every piece of legislation you work on can help. Overall, I had a very productive legislative session, which included tax reform and legislation to weatherize all the houses in Maine and half of businesses by 2030. I submitted legislation to create Pine Tree Economic Development Zones to encourage renewable-energy investment, which was rolled into a committee bill and is now helping boost economic investment in Maine. I sit on the VA Homeless Veterans Working Group and chair the Veterans Caucus. I was fortunate to pass legislation that made Maine one of the only states in the nation that allows any veteran to take advantage our quality higher education system at no cost, in conjunction with the 21st Century GI Bill. I also passed legislation to support homeless veterans and a bill that allows all veterans to enjoy Maine state parks, free of charge, and worked hard to ensure the establishment of the first memorial to women veterans in the State House Hall of Flags. A full listing can be found at www.alexcornell. org. I've worked closely with Republicans on veterans' issues, and all my bills were bipartisan.

Advice

STAY ENGAGED, KEEP AN OPEN MIND, and continue learning. If you stay in the conversation and contribute to it, you will be much more productive in getting legislation through and plans adopted. Make sure you are working with your supporters and other elected officials. One state senator in my area was vital in helping me learn the process and procedures of the Legislature.

Know the issues well. They can be gut-wrenching as you weigh them and try to do the best you can for different citizens of the region. When we're working on the budget, we do not like to see services and programs disbanded, so it is important to know where the real efficiencies are, so as to be truly fiscally responsible and not destroy key connections between the State and the community, especially in a difficult economic environment, where lives and livelihoods may be at stake.

It's great to find ways to help a constituent. I met a veteran, a sergeant, who had suffered a heart attack. He lost his job, and then he lost his health insurance, which spiraled into him losing his house. He is an example of why we need a national health-care program that is effective for America, to fix an outdated system that is not working. My staff and I did some research on veterans' benefits and found him a place to live. His situation had a happy ending, but unfortunately that is not the case for everyone.

You can never assume you are right on everything. During my campaign and in the work now, it has been critical not to view myself as a singular entity but as part of a community of individuals working for the same goal. And I make sure I hear everyone's opinions before I make a decision.

When we had a Democratic majority Legislature, we let the Republican bills get out of committee, to have a public hearing and be heard on the House and Senate floor. Now that we are in the minority, I hope we can continue to work in a bipartisan manner. In caucus, even around some of the more heated and controversial issues, we have become united because of the community we fostered within our caucus.

Stay active in your community through the education system or anything that is important to you. In my case, volunteering for Habitat for Humanity and coaching lacrosse and soccer at the junior high school have kept me in touch with my community. Most people respect that you are working hard and will be curious to talk about your story and why you want to be involved, even if they don't agree with you politically.

I live in Cobb County, Georgia. Some have given it the nickname Snob County. Our previous congressmen include renowned conservatives Newt Gingrich and Bob Barr. Historically, my district hasn't been the most receptive place for people of color. I mean, this is the place in Georgia where the last recorded lynching took place. When I told people I thought it was possible for me to win, they didn't believe me. But it's a county that is growing and open to change, a place I'm proud to represent and call home.

Alisha Thomas Morgan
Georgia House of Representatives

History

WHEN I WAS FOURTEEN, MY MOTHER forced me to go to a meeting of the NAACP (National Association for the Advancement of Colored People). Though she wouldn't have articulated it quite this way, she believed it was important to expose me to activities that would help me develop leadership skills. I took a book along, because I thought the meeting would be really boring, with a lot of old people sitting around.

But I was really inspired. I was quickly attracted to the Youth Council.

Young people were running their own meetings and talking about issues in the community. They had the ability within the organization to plan things they wanted; there was no "you're too young, let the adults handle that work" mentality. I think that has been the theme for me in terms of leadership all along—not waiting for someone to tell me I'm old enough to act, and grant me permission.

Politics

DURING COLLEGE I CONTINUED TO WORK with the NAACP through a variety of issues, such as juvenile justice, education, and affirmative action. I was involved in voter registration and empowerment. We were trying to get ten thousand eighteen- to thirty-five-year-olds registered and turned out to vote in 2001. We accomplished that goal in terms of registration, but we failed horribly when it came to actually getting them to vote.

I realized that people need a reason to get out and vote in an election. If they don't feel a connection with the process and their elected officials, they don't see a need to be involved. So I decided that there needed to be another step in voter empowerment. Elected officials who are connected to the people seemed to be the missing link.

I felt that there was a void in leadership in the community in which I lived. That's what inspired me to run for the state Legislature when I was twenty-two. I made the decision first and did the research later.

I decided to run as I was driving down the street after a panel discussion, during which I had said that I thought we needed a youth revolution and more young people standing on the front lines, as they have in every other movement we have seen in the world. The state Legislature was a place to impact the issues I cared about and to be an advocate and link for the community in the process. I thought I could get some things done.

Campaigning

I LIVE IN COBB COUNTY, GEORGIA. Some have given it the nickname Snob County. Our previous congressmen include renowned conservatives Newt Gingrich and Bob Barr. Historically, my district hasn't been the most receptive place for people of color. I mean, this is the place in Georgia where the last recorded lynching took place. When I told people I thought it was possible for me to win, they didn't believe me. But it's a county that is growing and open to change, a place I'm proud to represent and call home.

I was running against two men. I ran a strong, visible, grassroots campaign. But a former campaign consultant of mine decided he did not want to work with me any longer, and he put up another candidate in the race with the same last name.

Then he filed a residency challenge against me. I had lived in an apartment and then bought my first house in the same area. When reapportionment took place in Georgia in 2002, they ended up being in two different districts, so I wasn't given credit for continuous residency in my district. I went to court, where I lost my case.

This was all happening a month before the election. Absentee voting had already started, and my name wasn't on the ballot. But I kept knocking on doors and appealing to voters. I eventually won the court case on appeal and got back on the ballot. By that time, I had basically lost all of the absentee votes, but I still won the election with 65 percent of the vote.

I became the first African American legislator from Cobb County to serve in Georgia's General Assembly. Some would say my election was luck. Others would say it was divine.

I had a bad first year. First of all, I had to adjust to the fact that I was in a place where people didn't understand how I got there. How did a young, black woman get elected from Cobb County? And I was outspoken and passionate about progressive issues.

I was elected at the same time as our current governor, Sonny Perdue. He had made the centerpiece of his campaign returning the Confederate flag to the state Capitol. That stayed the headline issue during my first year.

Early on, I was invited to the Sons of Confederate Veterans meeting in my district. On the advice and counsel of one of my Republican colleagues, I took a member of the GBI (Georgia Bureau of Investigation) with me, because I wasn't sure what the outcome of the meeting was going to be. They had Confederate flags everywhere, sang *Dixie*, and berated the NAACP for taking up the issue of the Confederate flag. It was a bad situation, and I had to walk out, because I knew it was heading in the wrong direction, and I refused to be disrespected any longer. A lot of media were there, so that was the state of Georgia's introduction to me.

In 2004, my second year, the issue of gay marriage was on the ballot. I didn't really have a position on gay marriage at that time, but I did have a position on not discriminating against entire groups of people for political gain. I knew there were issues of fairness and equality involved.

Lots of members of my church had helped me get elected, and the church submitted a petition to ban gay marriage, taking a position that was in direct opposition to mine. That made for a tough re-election year. One of my opponents campaigned on that issue alone, distributing flyers throughout the community stating, "Alisha Morgan wants gay people to get married."

I was really afraid and concerned. I was getting phone calls from ministers and other people in the area, and everyone seemed mad about gay marriage. Some people who had voted for me and seemed pleased with what I had done as a legislator, said things like: You want gay people to get married, and I'm never voting for you again!

I remember calling the chairman of the Democratic Caucus from my front porch in tears, thinking that I might lose my election. I won handily, with 86 percent of the vote in the primary, and 56 percent in the general election. But at the time I didn't know how it was going to turn out.

In 2005 I had a run-in with the speaker of the House over the voter ID issue. With my personal history, voter empowerment has been very important to me. Georgia was instituting a policy of requiring voters to show a photo ID, which can be a barrier for people who are poor or elderly or students who don't have easy access to such an ID. The speaker was trying to silence me, and I refused to stop speaking out on the issue. He wanted a public apology, and there was discussion about expelling me from the Legislature. I didn't apologize, and I wasn't expelled, but it was a very intense time.

I would probably say that was the most difficult time in my life, because I had to understand the importance of standing on my convictions. That includes even when people who are your friends are not going to stand with you. Behind the scenes, people were telling me they were in support of me, but no one would talk to me on the House floor when I walked in.

People were afraid to associate with me, because I had "broken decorum." I felt like I was alone and raising hell on the floor, saying all the things other people were saying outside of meetings but didn't have the courage to say inside them. That was when I learned a very important lesson in life: Never apologize for who you are or what you believe in.

But then you realize that if you don't choose your battles—if you're not careful about relationships and trying to build bridges—you become isolated. That is what happened to me. I'm very thankful that we started the Young Elected Officials network that year.

When you're young and in public office, you feel like you're on an island. In many ways, you don't think anyone understands you. Everyone has lessons they think they need to teach you, and you are everyone's little niece or nephew. Don't get me wrong, I know we have things to learn. But sometimes you need to feel validated and be reminded that what you bring to the table is valuable. Age should not be a sign of qualification, but experience, desire, and courage.

I've really developed my personal leadership style over the last couple of years. I'm still outspoken, but I'm choosing my battles and finding issues in which I can work across the aisle. I'm developing relationships with legislators that can now see me as Alisha and not the "angry black woman." I have to say that I didn't see myself back then as an angry black woman, but it's the perception some had. I know better how to handle situations and have been much more effective in terms of getting bills passed.

I had a situation in which a very powerful representative came to me and presented a deal. If I supported him on his bill, he would take care of my budget priorities. Because I had been a young, ostracized activist, I had never before been in the game. No one had ever come to me to try to make a deal or approached me on a vote. So when he came to me, I really didn't know how to say what I knew I needed to say.

I consulted a wise mentor, who warned me about the dangers of making deals. He confirmed my commitment to vote for or against bills based on how I feel about the issues. You always do what you believe in and let the chips fall where they may. Because at some point, in the next session, there will always be something else that comes up, and you have to learn how to live for another day.

I'm dealing with a difficult situation now with labor unions. They are probably going to pull their support from me, because I support school vouchers. Until recently, I hated vouchers. What made me reconsider my position was a bill that for the first time would allow kids in chronically failing schools to transfer to private schools through vouchers.

I cannot in good conscience look into the eyes of a parent and say, "I know that your kid goes to a school that has been underperforming, and there are not any other public school options. I'm sorry, but he'll just have to stay there until we fix public education." I looked at the number of my colleagues whose kids are in private schools or in high-performing public schools because they can move to be near them. I believe in leveling the playing field, in equal opportunity for all people, in providing the same thing for every other child that I do for mine.

It's not that I support vouchers in general. I specifically support vouchers for low-income kids that are in grossly underperforming schools, because I think it's a crime for us as a legislative body to keep maintaining the status quo. The graduation rate among black and Hispanic males in Georgia is below 50 percent.

I respect teachers' unions and their interest is in protecting jobs. My job is about protecting kids and making sure they get a quality education. And unfortunately, when you talk about education reform, those two things compete. They should not have to, but they do.

We should start by allowing parents to choose where their children go to school. The zoned school for my daughter may be perfect for her, but if my neighbor across the street has different needs, why should he be stuck going to a school that does not meet his needs, even if it's great and performing well? Every child should be at a place that is safe and where he or she can thrive and have the best curriculum and tools available.

Advice

RECENTLY I WAS ON A PLANE, and I created a document I titled, "When This Is All Over, This Is What I Want to Have Happened." I asked myself several questions about my time in the Legislature and then wrote out lists of responses. How do I want to feel when this is over? What is it that I want to accomplish? What is it that I want people to think about me? What is it that I want to think about myself?

Several things became clear to me. First, you don't have to change your values for politics. Second, it's all about relationships and building bridges. And third, it's important not to say or do anything that has long-term consequences from which you can't recover.

If you are thinking about running for office because you're passionate and interested in service, and you have a wealth of experience in your community and are working on issues, then I think you're ready. Age and professional degrees are not determining factors. I believe there is a great opportunity now for young people who are willing to work across the aisle. I understand partisan politics, but I think it has been a hindrance to all of us. I think we need a new breed of elected officials, regardless of their age.

My dream is to become governor of Georgia. I'm thinking about that at thirty-one, and I'm sure there's someone out there thinking about running for public office at twenty-one. Don't wait. There is too much work to be done in our communities for us to wait for someone else to do it or for us to feel that someone needs to give us permission. It's time.

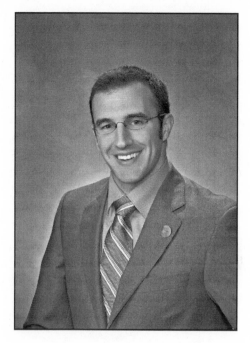

I walked into the local Democratic Party office. I'd just done an overnight shift at the hospital, so I was in my scrubs and looking very "doctorly"—and at age twenty-eight, very young as well. I said to the executive director, "Hello, I'm here to run for Congress. Just wanted to let you know. And by the way, how do I do that?"

Matt Heinz
Arizona House of Representatives

History

ELECTED OFFICE WAS NEVER EVER AN aspiration for me. Public speaking freaks me out. I do fine, but it's not something I envisioned for myself, and I'm still getting used to doing it.

What I responded to was the great need and pressure I see facing our country now and looming even larger on the horizon: a deteriorating and unsustainable health-care system. As a doctor, I saw it affecting all of my patients, nurses, partners, and colleagues.

I became a doctor believing that doctors should be stewards, main-taining the system for ourselves and future generations. We take an oath to do no harm. But if you don't have a system to care for the people you promised to take care of, then what good are you? You can't fulfill your obligation to society and the people you took an oath to help.

Throughout medical school, I continually observed that things were not going well for the people or the system. I had to smuggle drug samples to some of my indigent patients to make sure they did not have to go to the hospital, because there was no system in place for them. I encountered elderly patients who told me they did not take their medications every day, but sometimes every other day, or only once a week, because of the burden on their Social Security checks. I couldn't believe I was hearing these things from American citizens.

When I moved to Tucson for my residency in April 2003, it was more of the same. I saw more and more people in need of care in crowded hospital emergency rooms, and wait times of twelve to fourteen hours to see an ER doctor or to be admitted to the hospital. There was always an impending feeling of breakdown in the system, and I saw no one doing anything about it.

Politics

NONE OF OUR REPRESENTATIVES IN CONGRESS or from our area in the state Legislature were physicians, and our elected officials were not talking about the health-care problem. Occasionally you'd hear it mentioned in a speech, but it felt to me like giving lip service. And doing something is a lot different from talking about it.

In October 2005, the Republican congressman from my district in south Arizona decided to retire after twenty-two years in Congress. That caused an explosion of interest in people running for his seat. Meanwhile, I was writing up a storm to my friends about how ridiculous things are in the health-care system; about how it's falling apart and killing people. About half a dozen of them called me when they heard about the congressman's retirement, needling me and essentially saying: Why don't you just shut up and run for office?

Initially I reacted with: Fine, maybe I will! But I wasn't really thinking seriously about it. I mean, I was a no-name, who had just moved into the area. I had no network. I'd never done any public anything! At the time,

I was not even registered as a Democrat or Republican, but as a non-affiliated voter. If I decided to run, where would I go?

I decided to walk into the local Democratic Party office. It was kind of weird. I consider myself a true conservative on several issues, but I'm openly gay, for God's sake. I'm conservative in the sense that I don't think government should be meddling where it doesn't belong. Ironically I'm of a mind with Barry Goldwater, who said basically, "The gay thing—whatever!" And on abortion—well, my first floor speech in the Legislature was a five-minute talk about a woman's right to pursue her own health-care options in whatever way she feels necessary, which should be between, her, her physician, and her God. Barry Goldwater, thank you very much.

But I do think that health care is a state and national security issue, and there's a role for government in it. I believe that the "hand up" idea rather than the "handout" model is important. And I agree with the Democrats on a number of other policy issues that have been labeled socially progressive.

Medical care does not have to be 100 percent socialized or necessarily a single-payer system. But government should have a role. It's ridiculous to have close to 20 percent of our population without primary care, lacking knowledge about symptoms and treatments because there's no one to tell them, using emergency rooms for their basic care.

We are destroying our country by spending unnecessary billions to treat illnesses that could have been prevented. That is a national security crisis, because it is an economic drain. Look at our national debt and how much it is growing. The dollar is not going to be the international reference currency much longer, because it will become completely devalued.

Politically, we are already moving the way of Great Britain, a nice and marginally wealthy country, that doesn't really do anything—excuse me, Great Britain. We are going to be a retired superpower within the next two decades. And it will happen even faster if we continue to help China and India become world-dominating powers by having them loan us huge sums of money. It makes no fiscal sense to me to allow the health care drain to continue.

And, I mean, it's just not nice. Don't you want your neighbor to have his diabetic foot ulcer taken care of? Because, if not, he may have to have a foot amputation or end up in the intensive care unit—or dead. As a society, we are relatively neighborly folks; we don't want to see someone hurt or disadvantaged because of our direct or indirect action. The way things are now is not the way I grew up, and this is not the society I hope to live in. Giving everyone good health care is just the right thing to do.

So, I walked into the Democratic Party office in Tucson and said, "Hello, I'm here to run for Congress." The elderly woman volunteering at the front desk was startled and just said, "Ohhh . . ." That is apparently something that does not happen very often. Then she said, "Umm, let me get you our executive director."

I'd just done an overnight shift at the hospital, so I was in my scrubs and looking very "doctorly"—and at age 28, very young as well. I said to the executive director, "Hello, I'm here to run for Congress. Just wanted to let you know. And by the way, how do I do that?"

She was also a little puzzled. She said, "Let me let you talk to Martin." Martin Becall is an older man who's been in the party for many years. I have since cared for his one-hundred-year-old mother, and we are friends now. But at the time, I was a little perplexed by his immediate response. He said, "What! Who are you? You can't do that!"

I was like, What? That's like the most un-American response a person could give in that moment! And I don't take well to being told no. I'm the youngest and only male child in my family, so I'm used to getting what I want. I know that's bad, but I don't like hearing no, when I want to do something.

Then Martin said, "Why don't you become a precinct committee person?"

I thought, what the hell is that? No, no, no, dude. I'm a physician, and I'm pissed off about health care, and it's frustrating that we can't take care of people the way we need to, and it's going to bring down the country.

Okay, people don't seem to get that. Physicians tend to think in logical and problem-solving ways; we look at systems and how they interact with one another. So I told him, "By God, I don't know anything about the state or federal government, but I can learn *really* fast, and then I can contribute." I ultimately decided not to run for Congress at that time, but shortly thereafter ran for a seat in the Arizona House of Representatives.

Campaigning

I WALKED DOOR TO DOOR. I could write a book about my neighborhood, which is partly older white and conservative and partly Catholic and Hispanic, with a strong LGBT [lesbian, gay, bisexual, transgender] community. I live in a diverse district with diverse needs, but in every sector and quadrant, people wanted to talk with me about health care. I would just say that I'm running for office and I'm a physician, and then I didn't have to say another word.

One guy showed me his red, swollen ankle and asked, "What do you think this is?" I told him it could be osteoarthritis, or gout if he was prone to it. The guy responded, "By God, you *are* a doctor! That's exactly what it is, osteoarthritis. I'm voting for you!"

Going door to door, you only have two or three minutes with constituents to make an impression. I had a sheet of paper telling me who I was looking for, their party registration, how often they voted— basically a cheat sheet. One day I was looking for a woman I'll call Betty, who was seventy-four years old. A woman in her forties answered the door, and I was a little surprised. "Hi, I'm looking for Betty," I said cheerfully. Then I heard a wet, nasty, terrible coughing sound from a sofa back in the living room. "That sounds awful," I said. The woman at the door responded that that was her mom, Betty, in the back.

I told her I didn't want to pry, but I mentioned that I was a doctor and asked if there was anything I could do to help. She seemed startled at first but then appreciative. I got a message a week later from Betty, thanking me for my concern and generosity and letting me know that she had told all her neighbors about me. That was not just good politics, but the response of a caring physician.

Advice

MY ADVICE TO OTHER YOUNG POLITICIANS is don't take politics or yourself too seriously, or you'll go crazy. Like most states, Arizona has budget problems, and we are highly fractured, with divisions on all sides. The work we do as legislators is important. So work hard and diligently, but don't let situations drive you nuts.

Trust is your most valuable currency. Trust and relationships. Whether it is a lobbyist or the speaker of the House, the relationships you build are crucial, because that's how you get stuff done. The reason I have two Republican cosponsors on my health-reform bill is that I'm a physician, but also because I'm a reasonable guy.

If you want to run for office, do it. Then do it again. Don't get discouraged. I lost my first race for Arizona House District 28, but I impressed city leaders and citizens in the community even in losing. I developed a great network of supporters that helped me get elected in House District 29. People listened to what I was saying and helped lay the foundation for a successful campaign, and I unseated the incumbent in the primary. If you feel like you have a calling and need to do it— you're exactly the kind of person we need.

Climate change is about justice, about having a world—and leaving one for future generations—that allows us all to live our lives with dignity and respect. With the exception of astronauts in outer space, all of human societal interactions exist entirely within the confines of our planet and its biosphere. And that is incredibly fragile. We are running into limits in our ability to continue polluting and extracting resources in ways that are harming our home. We have only one planet. As young people, we are the ones who will have to live with the consequences of the decisions being made today. If we do not address these big global issues, then all of our work will be undone.

Dominic Frongillo
Town Council, Caroline, New York

History

I GREW UP ON A DIRT road in the small, rural town of Caroline in Upstate New York. I recently moved out of my childhood home with a beautiful landscape near a state forest. When I was young, my mom often took me on walks up and down our road. We would pick up trash, and she would point out things: "Do you see that? There is erosion right there. It's important that we protect our land and our farms." I gained a sense of stewardship at an early age.

I never thought I would run for office, although there was an indication of that possibility when I was in eleventh grade. My history class participated in Congress in Action, and all the students played the roles of members of Congress. I was Sherwood Boehlert, a moderate Republican, and my issue was Mars exploration. This was soon after NASA had lost two Mars rovers: one blew up in the atmosphere, and the other landed on Mars but was never heard from. I made the case for continued funding of planetary exploration.

I dressed up in a three-piece suit and gave an impassioned speech to my fellow students in our gymnasium. My best line was, "People say, How could NASA mess up and lose two Mars rovers?—it's not like it's rocket science. But, it *is* rocket science, and let's not forget that!"

When I was in high school, I had the opportunity to work with a local city planner in the City of Ithaca. I shadowed him to brainstorming sessions with middle-school students, where he asked the kids to imagine what they wanted their neighborhoods to be like. They responded with things like, "I want a skateboard park," or "I want stores that serve kids." I thought it was great to actually ask people, even middle-school students, to help shape their neighborhoods' future. I learned that this approach is called "community visioning," or "participatory planning." In short, it's democracy: giving people a direct say in what they want their communities to be like.

After high school, I went to the University of Rochester and then transferred to Cornell University, where I pursued an independent degree with honors in sustainable community development. I was interested in community and in solving problems at a local level. One day I saw an ad in the paper announcing that the Town of Caroline was seeking applicants to the Planning Board. My father encouraged me to contact our town supervisor.

I was very nervous, but I asked him if there was any way I could get involved in the town's planning effort. Town officials had just formed a planning board, and I ended up being an intern for the board. Citizens of Caroline, approximately thirty volunteers, wrote the plan, and the board's job was to put it together in a way that was cohesive. I helped put together the pieces. The contents of the plan included a walkable and safe community, vibrant hamlets and mixed-use areas, and preservation of our beautiful forests and open spaces. I found the process amazing and incredibly empowering, seeing citizens literally writing the vision and comprehensive plan for their community.

Politics

AT ONE OF OUR MEETINGS, THE deputy town supervisor and the chair of the local Democratic Party cornered me and said, "Dominic, have you ever considered running for Town Council? We think you'd be great." I had never considered it, and my first thought was, *Why would I ever want to do that?* I said no thank you. But they kept urging me to reconsider.

It was a real struggle for me. It was the summer of 2005, and I had just graduated from college. I was really interested in seeing the world and understanding what it would be like to live deeply in a community. Growing up, I was busy with schoolwork and felt that I didn't have the connections and deep rootedness in my community.

I thought about going into the Peace Corps in a Latin American country, to learn Spanish and to "find myself." But the more I thought about it, the more I realized I could do what I hoped for in my own hometown. A lot of people in New York leave their counties or the state to find opportunities. I realized I had the opportunity to make a difference as a change agent, to build something positive and to find myself in my own community. I decided to run.

Campaigning

THERE WERE FOUR PEOPLE RUNNING FOR two open seats. The other Democrat and I printed up flyers and split up the town. I took the more rural areas. Sometimes I borrowed my parents' van, but usually I rode my bicycle—even once during a hailstorm. I knocked on a lot of doors. I just said to people who answered, "Hi, my name is Dominic, and I live over on Bailor Road, and I'm running for Town Council, and I want to know what your thoughts are about the future of the town."

I was struck by how few people have ever actually had a politician come to their door. People would say, Really? You're coming to my door?

Especially at the places down a rural dirt road in the middle of nowhere with no other houses around, they would say, No one has ever taken the time to come to my door before.

I found it incredibly inspiring that I had the ability to engage people in the political process in a way that they had never been engaged before. When I asked them what they wanted to see in the town, initially many were silent, because they had never been asked that question. Then they would open up and talk about the issues that were important to them and that they felt passionate about. I learned so much from just listening to citizens.

Caroline is in the northern reaches of Appalachia, and I discovered an economic situation going on in my community quite different from what many people are used to. It was new for me to approach houses with broken windows and scrap metal in the yard, but I made it my mission during the campaign to value everyone, no matter what their circumstances or party affiliation. One man, who was missing a couple of teeth and obviously hadn't showered in quite a while, was particularly moved that I had come to his door and valued his opinion about the town. He thought about it and gave a very good answer about a vision that he had for the community, and we had a good conversation. I learned how important it is to engage everyone equally, to value his thoughts as much as I did the opinions of the Cornell professors I had met.

I was surprised when I learned that I was the top vote getter of the four candidates. I took that as a message that people really appreciate that you just show up at their door. On election night, I was with Democratic Party members, elected officials and election observers. The tallies came in, and we had a clean sweep. That was the first time in history that all five members of the Town Council were Democrats. A dozen years ago, there was not a single Democrat in office in Caroline.

I'm both an elected and an appointed official. I was elected to the Town Council at twenty-two years old and then appointed to the position of deputy town supervisor. I'm pretty sure I'm the youngest in the history of Tompkins County.

My colleagues and I wanted to tap into rural values that everyone could get behind, which is a challenge, given the mix of people in the area and the tension that creates. There are two major segments in our town. One is the "old-timers": the people who live on the roads named after their families because their ancestors lived there generations ago. The other is the "newcomers," which includes those who commute to work at Cornell and other places in Ithaca.

I am former chair of an inter-municipal collaboration called the Recreation Partnership, dedicated to ensuring that young people have access to programs. I helped a local charter school get up and going, and I've worked in development and nutrition with the county's Planning Department. But my greatest passion is the environment. I am fortunate to work as a community energy educator with Cornell Cooperative Extension of Tompkins County.

My interest in energy comes from the idea that saving it benefits local communities and households, improving air quality and saving money that can be reinvested in the local economy. And becoming less dependent upon foreign oil improves our economic and national security.

Projections about climate change are constantly worsening, based on what we actually see with carbon emissions going up, sea levels rising, and other indicators such as the Arctic ice melting. I realize that if I really want to make a lasting difference in my community, I need to see what is affecting it and think ahead, taking seriously my sense of stewardship and responsibility for the town of Caroline. If we do not address these big global issues, then all of our work will be undone.

Our Town Council is working with other communities to strengthen our collaboration around these concerns. Our county's Greenhouse Gas Committee received a statewide award for its comprehensive plan calling for and outlining an 80 percent reduction of carbon emissions by 2050.

I helped to found Energy Independent Caroline. We made it an official advisory committee of the town and started working on community outreach. I took on the website, trying to increase public information and participation. I started an email list, which for the first time in the town's history has enabled citizens to get notices, updates, and agendas of meetings. We have more than one-sixth of the entire town on the list, which is impressive for a small town.

Energy Independent Caroline has been very successful. On April 19, 2008, one hundred volunteers went door to door—by foot, bicycle, hybrid car, and horseback—and delivered fourteen hundred energy-efficient light bulbs, one to every home in Caroline, across fifty-five square miles in three hours. People had heard about the Lighten Up Caroline event and were really excited, many of them waiting at their doors when we arrived. Although it's been done in urban areas, it was a challenge with all our dirt roads. But we pulled off the largest single-day distribution of energy-saving light bulbs in rural Upstate New York.

As young people, we are the ones who will have to live with the consequences of the decisions being made today. It is absolutely critical that young people have a strong voice at the table. That's why I made sure that I went to the United Nations climate negotiations in Bali, Copenhagen, and Cancun.

I learned that if you just showed up and had your badge on, government ministers from other countries would come up to you, because they assumed you were someone important. The environment minister from Uganda handed me his business card. I didn't know what to do with it.

What I learned in those meetings is the power of young people, who had the ability to move some of the most powerful people in the world—not just through facts and figures, but through stories. The younger the speaker, the more impact they seemed to have. It was amazing to see the power of a seven-year-old talking to a government minister about why she's so passionate about protecting the land, and the air, and the water.

Young people can speak their positive vision and inspire people in a way that is powerful. They can tell a story that moves those high-ranking officials and connects with them emotionally in a way that they are normally not impacted by other delegates. Adults see the future when they look at young people and awaken to the moral sense that they are inheriting what the current generation leaves behind.

At the Bali climate negotiations, a space was created for hundreds of youths from around the world to gather and share stories. The Americans would get up and say that they were organizing on college campuses and writing letters to their senators. Then the Australians would stand up and say, "We took over a coal plant last month and got national media attention for shutting it down." And the Americans would say, "Well, if we did that, we would be arrested on terrorism charges."

One unforgettable story was from Claire, a woman in her early twenties from Kiribati, a small island in the South Pacific. She stood up and said, "My island is just a meter above sea level. My family is very worried, and we do not know what we are going to do if sea levels rise. We don't know where we are going to go. For many years I felt so alone, believing that no one cared." With tears in her eyes, she said that at the conference she felt for the first time that she was not alone and that people care. She brought the room to tears.

A delegate from the African nation of Togo came up to me and asked, "Do not Americans care? Do not they care about the melting glaciers and the encroaching deserts? Do not they care about what is happening in the world?" I could only say that there is a growing movement, especially among young people, awakening to our responsibility and our interconnection with the rest of the world.

Climate change for me now is about justice, about having a world—and leaving one for future generations—that allows us all to live our lives with dignity and respect. I was grateful to discover a national network of young people for sustainable development who share this view. It is SustainUs.org. The network sends groups of U.S. youth to international conferences on sustainable development. These are important conferences, because their work will replace the Kyoto Protocol that now governs global climate change issues.

With the exception of astronauts in outer space, all of human societal interactions exist entirely within the confines of our planet and its biosphere. And that is limited and incredibly fragile. It is a miracle that we have the abundance of life that is provided to us on earth, and we are running into very basic physical limits in our ability to continue polluting and extracting resources in ways that are harming our home. We have only one planet.

For me this is the fundamental challenge: how are we going to improve quality of life and make sure everyone has access to education, healthy and walkable communities, basic water and sanitation, and the ability to achieve their own dreams? And how can we ensure that in a way that doesn't compromise future generations?

In Copenhagen young people wore T-shirts that said, HOW OLD WILL YOU BE IN 2050?" One of the youths met Gordon Brown, prime minister of the U.K. He burst out laughing, because he realized that he'd be dead in 2050. But the young people at the conference will be around, and we will live with the consequences of the decisions being made now. Young people are asking, what kind of world are we leaving for our children and their grandchildren?

Advice

I HAVE A REALLY STRONG INTEREST in seeing other young people run for office. The most important thing is for every young person to look and see how they can get engaged in their own community. It's crucial to find a reason to go out and talk to people, making connections and building relationships.

I've learned so much from Don Barber, our town supervisor. He's a farmer who gets up every day at 5:30 to milk the cows and take the horses out, whose father served on the Town Council before him. One of the most important things I've learned from him is the importance of having an open and collaborative process for decision making, making sure that everyone at every meeting has all the necessary information and an opportunity to participate. The process defines how effective each decision becomes.

Don literally turned around town government when he became town supervisor. At that time, members of the Town Council had their backs to the public at their meetings. The first thing he did was turn the Council around to face the public. And his institution of advisory boards has dramatically increased the participation of people in town and given them a direct voice in policy. Now we have a network of people working together to try to do the right thing.

It's critical to take people's concerns seriously. I remember that several years ago there was a problem with a bridge that was in danger of washing out. I called the county Highway Department and reported it. I was young and talking to a government official and really nervous, but the guy on the phone was so nice and engaged.

Eight years later, I look back on that moment and realize that one person really made an effort to be something other than another government bureaucrat. I really valued that, and now I wish I could call him back and tell him how much I appreciated it. It's very important to appreciate public servants.

Probably the funniest advice I've received was from a Town Council member from another town, whom I met at the New York Association of Town Meetings. He told me, "Don't you ever forget that the lowest form of life in town government is a Town Council member." When I asked him what he meant, he explained, "Town clerks are incredibly important—they take the minutes, and they can make you look bad, so make sure you're nice to them. So is the person who cleans the bathrooms in the Town Hall—because they get paid!" Then he said again with a wry smile, "The lowest form of life in town government is the Town Council member. But—if you combine three Town Council members, you just created the highest form of life in town government, because they can pass laws! Don't you forget it."

When my predecessor asked me about running for his seat, I chuckled, "Are you crazy! Not only do I have an ethnic name, but I'm also of Muslim faith." It's not just that people didn't recognize my last name, they couldn't pronounce it. And the way it is pronounced—"Ta-leeb"—is very close to the most controversial terrorist group in the world.

Rashida H. Tlaib
Michigan House of Representatives

History

I'M THE ELDEST OF FOURTEEN CHILDREN, with seven younger brothers and six younger sisters. Both my parents are immigrants from Palestine. I grew up among Arab Americans who were generous, loyal, and lavish with their food and emotions.

If it weren't for Islam and what it brought to me in my early life, I don't think I would have the strength I have today. It is one of those peaceful religions, but it's disappointing people don't see that side. And many people seem to think that all Arab Americans just got off a boat, not recognizing our many contributions to this country.

I was raised in an exciting, diverse, and growing immigrant community in southwest Detroit. I went to a high school that was predominantly African American. There were also Latinos and whites, but only about ten other Arab American students.

Being Arab American and Muslim, part of a minority in a community that's so ethnically diverse, I didn't really fit in. But at the same time, I fit in everywhere. I learned to get along with everybody. I saw things through the eyes of different cultures, and that has made me a better American and a better legislator.

I went to school with a lot of undocumented students, and many of them didn't even know what it meant to have legal immigration status. But when we all started applying for colleges in our junior and senior years of high school, they began to realize they did not have Social Security numbers. I heard things like, "There is this wall I can't cross. I can't go on to school."

I was not really politically involved at that stage. My father was a worker at the Ford plant and was a member of the UAW (United Auto Workers union). When I turned eighteen, he told me, "Vote, vote, vote!" Our family would make a trip out of going to the polls during elections. That was about as civically engaged as we were. I didn't even know the names of my state representative or state senators at the time.

Politics

FAST-FORWARD SEVERAL YEARS. I WAS working at nonprofit organizations and putting myself through law school. And I heard about this new state representative who had introduced a bill to provide in-state tuition at Michigan universities for all undocumented students. I thought, "This is amazing, and this is so great!"

So I looked him up. Steve Tobocman, a Jewish man who represented southwest Detroit, had worked a lot on community development initiatives. As a lawyer, he had set up a nonprofit organization called Community and Legal Resources.

His work led him to run for public office. He unseated an incumbent doing door-to-door, direct voter contact. I believe southwest Detroit had never had a candidate actually go door to door in the way he did. I volunteered for his campaign and knocked on doors with him a few times.

I worked for six years with ACCESS, which is the largest Arab American human service agency in the country. I did immigration advocacy post-9/11, when issues of fear and hostility toward Muslims and Arab Americans were surfacing with intensity. ACCESS needed someone on the ground in Michigan, educating people at the state level, as well as working with our congressional delegation.

In his last term, Steve Tobocman was elected Majority House Leader and needed to expand his staff. He approached me about it. At first I resisted, but then I realized that it was just the right place and time for me. I knew that in two years I could get to know the inside of the political system better. And in the post-9/11 climate, we were facing English-only legislation, designations of "citizen" on drivers' licenses, the requirement of a Social Security number to get a marriage license, and other issues that were creating barriers for many foreign nationals, legal or not. So I jumped aboard.

Within two months of my starting on Steve's staff, he sat me down and asked me what I was going to do in two years. I told him that I would probably go back to the nonprofit world and continue my work there. He asked me what I thought about running for his seat, and I chuckled, "Are you crazy! Come on, Steve, *not only do I have an ethnic name, but I'm also of Muslim faith.*"

He tried to encourage me, but I said no emphatically. It was a definite no! But whenever people asked Steve who was running for his seat, he told them that he really wanted me to do it, and their response was consistently positive. I guess you could say he started a coup.

Dave Woodward was a friend and the Michigan director of the Center for Progressive Leaders. The organization calls folks together for meetings, and at a certain point we always divide ourselves into those who want to work on issue or elections campaigns. I would usually go to the area for issue campaigning, carrying my concern for immigration reform.

At a session in Kalamazoo, Michigan, when I was sitting in the "issues" section, Dave came up and kissed me on the cheek, and then said, "You are my pet project this week."

I said, "Whoa—Steve talked to you, too?"

Dave said, "You are making a mistake." He told me to leave that section and go sit with the candidates. I said no, and he looked at me and said, "Get over there. It's the same as being over here." But I did not listen.

On the last day of the session, Shelly Weisburg, a staffer at ACLU-

Michigan, came over and finally made it clear for me. She knew that I had been in the caucus room when representatives were discussing drivers' licenses, because Steve had invited me to talk during that debate in the Michigan Legislature. In the end, the legislators voted for something that was not as bad as it could have been.

"Rashida, imagine that you were not in the room when they talked about drivers' licenses," Shelly said to me. "People like us never think about running for office, and that's what's wrong with the system." And that's when it clicked.

We were already supporting a candidate who was an immigrant, but he wasn't very aggressive in campaigning. I decided that I would run only if he dropped out of the race, which I had a hint he was going to do. Eight days before the filing deadline, I dropped my name as a candidate.

Campaigning

PARTICULARLY IN DETROIT POLITICS, NAME RECOGNITION is so important. We have people who run five or six times before they get elected. They just run and keep running, to get their names out there. It's that way in the Middle East, too. It's all about the name of your father.

It's not just that people didn't recognize my last name, they couldn't pronounce it. And the way it is pronounced—"Ta-leeb"—is very close to the most controversial terrorist group in the world. So, I didn't have the name recognition, and I didn't have any money for the race.

In southwest Detroit, which is arguably the most diverse part of Michigan, we have at least twenty different ethnicities, from all over South and Central America and the Middle East, along with Romanians. The last census tract states that my district, which is the only part of Detroit that is actually growing in population, is about 45 percent Latino, 35 percent African American, and 8 percent white. Two percent of the district is Arab American. So when I ran for office, people thought I was crazy because I'm not Latino or African American.

Our campaign theme was "Southwest Detroit's Own—Strength, Talent, and Diversity Working for Us." It was intense. There were seven people running against me: four African Americans and three Latinos. And here I am, Middle Eastern and, oh, yeah, by the way, also a Muslim. Only one other Muslim woman had been elected to any state Legislature in America, and no Muslim woman had ever served in the Michigan Legislature.

Steve told me to focus on two things: doors and dollars. So I sent out this little card telling people I was coming to visit, with a picture of me shaking someone's hand, and I got out there. What was exciting was when I started showing up, people said things like, "You actually came!"

They were so fascinated. A lot of people asked if I'm Indian. When I told them that I'm Arab American, they'd usually ask, "Are you Muslim?" To my surprise, I got responses like, "Ohhh—cool." That was nice. That was a blessing.

People couldn't figure me out. I would share that I grew up in south-west Detroit, went to high school here, and worked full-time through school. I told them that I didn't speak English until I started school, and that if it hadn't been for the bilingual program that helped my parents understand public education—with my mother's eighth-grade education and my father's fourth-grade education—things might be different for us. I just shared my story, and it resonated.

People loved the fact that I'm the eldest of fourteen, especially my seniors who come from large families. They also loved that I'm young and passionate. One of the things I told potential constituents was that direct service and advocacy would go hand and hand with legislation in my office.

I tell my Muslim supporters that I ran a campaign the same way that we pray—peacefully and with determination. We pray five times a day. Since I've become a legislator, I've had to call my Imam and say, "I'm missing my prayers a lot, but I'm making them up." He tells me, "Make them up when you can, Rashida. God will understand."

The time I take to pray helps me to stay calm when things are chaotic, and helps me to understand my role. I have 109 colleagues in the Michigan Legislature, and many of them had never met a Muslim. While I think that's shocking and sad, it has also made me a better Muslim.

The Islam concept of charity is that you take care of your home, and then once you do that, you go and take care of the most vulnerable out there in the world. That's the whole point of being compassionate. I know that getting people through every day is just as important as legislation, which can take years to implement and may not ever touch a life as much as direct service.

I'm the only state legislator in Michigan with a Neighborhood Service Center. A big sign lets people know that this is where they can come for legal and other services. I know that I am serving a predominantly non-Muslim area through my service, and that's kind of cool.

Detroit's City Council is not elected by district, so I'm the only elected official representing southwest Detroit. I want to be the community partner of my constituents. I had one resident say to me, "You are governor and mayor, council member and state representative."

I periodically meet with all the city directors, and I have created a resource guide toward creating a partnership. I encourage my residents to call them if there is a problem, and then I will call too as their state representative. That increases the chances of having issues such as illegal dumping addressed by a city official. I almost feel like I'm running a nonprofit organization as a state representative.

But most important, I have learned that I have the "power to convene." Though I had been the program director of a nonprofit and a legislative staffer, it was hard for me at first to understand the office of being a state representative. I knew that I had to make the decisions, but I didn't really understand the authority that I had.

Now I have resources and tools that I never had access to as an organizer and advocate, or even as a nonprofit lawyer. For example, I brought together members of the EPA (Environmental Protection Agency) with different groups to get them to work together. It was powerful. We stopped a billionaire from illegally building a bridge. People were like, "There is no way you're going to stop him." But I initiated a conversation and sent information to officials of the U.S. Coast Guard who listened and helped too, and we eventually did.

I've picked up the work that Steve Tobocman started, going from school to school to raise support for undocumented students. His bill allowing anyone who graduates from a Michigan high school access to higher education was found to be unconstitutional, because the state is not allowed to legislate universities. In retrospect, we realized that state monies could be tied to in-state tuition through appropriations, and that's the way we're trying to proceed now.

My main message to my colleagues is that our immigration system is incredibly broken. I can't emphasize enough how deteriorated it is. Not only is it not working for the business community, it's not working for families, and it's not working for America.

It feels like we're going after the victims of a broken immigration system. It is our fault that they're here, driven to desperation by our own government and economic policies. It is our fault that many U.S. citizens married to undocumented spouses can't be reunited. It is our fault that we have an underground way of hiring undocumented workers, because we don't have a system that works for the demand as needed. It is our fault, because we have a system that does not work for anyone.

It's been twenty years since we've overhauled our immigration system. It is appalling and unbelievable to me that people don't understand that going after the people who are the victims of our failure is not fixing the problem. That is simply going to cost us a lot of money and tear up our country.

Let's stop the talk about "just having them get in line." The problem is that there is no line. I can't tell you how many good people end up in this tragic mix and are gone—and they're people who deserve to be here. Let's target the core problems instead of the victims.

Advice

I ASK PEOPLE INTERESTED IN RUNNING for public office why they want to serve, and what they want to change in their communities. In order to serve well, you have to develop a sincere connection to your community so strong that you will be a good public servant. If you just want to run for public office, that's not good enough. You have to be truly invested in the community.

It's important not just to go to the meetings with those whom you know or to surround yourself with all the people who are supporting you. You have to get out there in a grassroots way in a community you absolutely love and where you are dedicated to improving the quality of life for its residents. And then, you have to go connect with everybody. It has to be intimate, and it has to be personal.

During my debate with John McCain, he was standing across from me saying negative things about health-care reform. I looked at him and said, "John, I find it ironic that a guy who has been on government-run health care since the day you were born, and will be on government-run health care until the day you die, opposes health-care reform for everyone else." It was a pretty spectacular experience.

Rodney Glassman
City Council, Tucson, Arizona

History

I GREW UP IN FRESNO, CALIFORNIA. My mom and dad, who were involved in a number of charitable organizations, gave me a profound sense of service. And so did the local Boy Scouts. I was fortunate enough to become an Eagle Scout at the age of thirteen.

I come from a family of lifelong learners. My parents instilled in me the importance of always working, as well as the value of getting a very good education and always continuing to learn. I have a BA, MBA, MPA, PhD, and JD—and I'm thirty-two years old.

I first attended Cornell University for my freshman year of college. Then at age nineteen, I moved to Tucson to manage Gateway Ice Center, an ice-skating rink that was part of our family business, while I attended the University of Arizona. As a small-business person, I got involved with the Tucson community, joining the board of the Boy Scouts and participating in the Jewish community. I had my first interactions with local elected officials and saw that they were utilizing their positions as leaders in the community to shine a light on the organizations and issues that I thought were the most important.

Politics

DURING THIS TIME, I VOLUNTEERED ON the campaign of Raul Grijalva, who left our County Board of Supervisors to run for Congress. When my family sold our business in 2003, I went to Washington to work for Congressman Grijalva. I had the choice of getting a PhD at George Washington University, or getting a PhD in Arid Land Resource Sciences at the University of Arizona. I missed Arizona, so I came home and kept my job with the congressman, working as a legislative aide for business and agriculture. I picked up my PhD and took another job as a consultant for a company called KB Homes, which at the time was the largest home builder in southern Arizona, and got accepted into law school.

The city councilwoman for my area decided she did not want to run for reelection. I got a call from my friend who is in Congress, Gabrielle Giffords, who asked if I would consider running for the seat. I talked to my boss, Congressman Grijalva, and he liked the idea. I talked to my other boss at KB Homes and he also liked the idea. So I thought it would be a natural extension of the community work I was already doing.

Campaigning

I ran a very unique campaign. I decided not to accept anything over a twenty-dollar contribution from anyone. I collected 2,320 contributions. I had hundreds of people who had never participated in the political process before because they had never been asked. It was really powerful for me to see that people really want to be engaged if they are approached about participating.

Another thing that was rewarding and interesting was having house parties where people got to know each other, and, more importantly, where people who had not participated in such activities were able to get engaged. What I learned from the first campaign was the importance of engaging everyone in the process—from young to old, businesspeople to environmentalists. Politics historically has not provided an opportunity for everyone.

I campaigned with the energy of a concert singer and the spirit of a hockey player. I campaigned like I serve—which is, I value every person and all feedback. I was a Jewish boy in a Mormon Boy Scout troop, who attended a Catholic high school and married a nice Jewish girl in law school. I'm a conservative Democrat who worked for one of the most liberal members of Congress for four years.

I campaigned with the goal of giving everyone a seat at the table, and that was how I was able to get elected at the age of twenty-nine to the Tucson City Council with more than 60 percent of the vote. I received support and endorsements, from the Sierra Club to Planned Parenthood to the Chamber of Commerce and the Tucson Association of Realtors.

In Arizona, job creation, education, and environmental sustainability related to water and other natural resources are very important issues. All three relate to the future of our state. My major accomplishment on the City Council is passing the first rainwater-harvesting ordinance for commercial development in the country.

"Go with your gut" has been some of the best political advice I've ever been given. Since I've been on City Council, I've lost about sixty pounds, so there's a lot less gut to go with. When I went to sign up for Air Force JAG training, I was told I needed either to grow four inches or lose the sixty pounds. Let's just say I stopped eating so much.

I had a client, a retired Air Force member, who came to my office on the military base one day to get his will done. He looked at my nametag, then at me, and back at the nametag. He said, "I have a councilman named Glassman."

I responded, "Yes, that's me!"

He said, "No, no. This guy came by my house during the campaign. He was much heavier!"

I think going door to door is so important, because it provides constituents the opportunity to get to know candidates and give feedback.

To this day, I still have friends and supporters that I met just walking door to door, who were excited and willing to support me and still feel comfortable calling me and sharing their ideas.

One practice I have is that I remind people that they can always call me if they need a trashcan. Council members can do so much for the big picture, but I always ask my colleagues, when was the last time you tried to wheel your trashcan down to the street with one of its wheels broken? That is pretty hard to do.

So, even the little things that we can do to help people are so important. That is why it's such a wonderful job I have, because I literally spend my time helping people. I love it. And I'm grateful that I also had the opportunity to start a foundation in 2003. I've been able to raise quite a bit of money through it for nonprofits that serve children.

I was in Air Force JAG training in Alabama when Attorney General Terry Goddard called and asked if I would explore the 2010 U.S. Senate race. In the past twenty years, Arizona really hadn't had a candidate to run against John McCain. Because I wanted to see if Arizonans were interested in the choice and wanted everyone to be able to voice their opinions, I chose, as with my City Council race, not to accept any more than twenty dollars from anyone.

Arizonans are hurting, and they don't want to support a candidate who will just go back to Washington and support Democratic ideas or oppose Republican ones. They want to support candidates who champion quality ideas and want to move Arizona forward. I don't care if you are a member of the Tea or coffee party—what I care about is that you care about the future of our state. I wanted to do in the U.S. Senate what I have done on the Tucson City Council, which is use consensus building to bring people together to work for Arizona's future.

I had a very tough four-way primary election, because I was not going to pander to one particular group; I stayed focused on what I thought was the right thing for Arizona. When it came to the general election, I was really about staying focused on the positive. I ran a very positive campaign. Our commercials, speeches, and news articles were all positive. We were critical of McCain's record but never attacked him personally.

The number-one issue in Arizona during the campaign was jobs—jobs and keeping tax dollars here in Arizona. McCain has a reputation for not bringing our taxpayer dollars home. The average state gets $50 per person in federal projects, and Arizona gets about $15 per person. It is those tax dollars coming back into print shops and restaurants that creates jobs.

We were in the middle of debate about the SB 1070 immigration bill during the election, which had many groups labeling Arizona anti-immigrant and calling for a boycott of the state. I was busy saying don't boycott Arizona; come here, because we need your money. SB 1070 was a giant distraction that could have derailed the Democratic Party nationally, because Democrats were so busy justifying why they didn't support the Arizona bill that they didn't have time to talk about the issues that people actually care about.

The funniest story of my Senate campaign happened in Kingman, Arizona. The night before an event there, my young volunteers were setting up and met a woman and asked for her support. She started yelling about what a horrible person I was.

So I showed up the next day in Kingman and had a really nice conversation with the lady, before telling her who I was. We finally got around to introducing ourselves. When I told her I was Rodney Glassman, she told me I was a nightmare of a guy when I was nineteen years old and running the skating rink. She said, "What happened to you?"

I smiled and told her I had grown up. "I'm thirty-two years old now." She ended up being a really great supporter.

One of the most enlightening moments of the campaign came when I was in Graham County and met a waitress named Tracey. She had quit her job as a prison guard the same day that her child was not served lunch at his school when his lunch ticket was a quarter short and he couldn't call her because she was at work. That moment provided an example to me that many hard-working families are struggling so close to the margins.

Another memorable moment was when I got to debate John McCain. He was standing across from me saying negative things about health-care reform. I looked at him and said, "John, I find it ironic that a guy who has been on government-run health care since the day you were born, and will be on government-run health care until the day you die, opposes health-care reform for everyone else." It was a pretty spectacular experience.

During the debate, a newscaster who was moderating said to McCain, "Carl Hayden brought the Central Arizona Project and Barry Goldwater brought the GI Bill. After a twenty-year history in Washington, DC, what is your legislative legacy?"

McCain answered, "Honesty and straight talk." The next day he started attacking me. He accused me of plagiarizing my PhD dissertation, which is obviously ridiculous. He accused me of being liberal because I worked for Congressman Raul Grijalva. He sent out postcards saying I would be bad for immigration reform. Anytime he felt threatened, he would attack.

Jobs, education, and immigration reform were the main issues in my campaign. Jobs were my top issue, and I wanted to make Arizona the solar capital of the world. I also wanted to create a federal tax code and incentives to keep our tax dollars and jobs in the United States rather than sending them overseas. On education, I wanted to increase our per-pupil spending and decrease our student-to-teacher ratio. On immigration reform, I favored securing the border, initiating a guest worker program, and figuring out what we are going to do with the eleven or twelve million immigrants who are already here.

The biggest stumbling block I had in my U.S. Senate race was that I spent $1.2 million and John McCain had $32 million to spend. I was the Planned Parenthood, labor, environment, education, and small-business candidate in that election. We had lots of organizational support, but we did not have the millions of dollars to fund our campaign that comes from being an incumbent and a failed presidential nominee.

I will always be grateful for the diversity of people and experiences that came my way during the campaign. My campaign treasurer was also the state treasurer of the Tucson branch of the Mormon Church. I think I sang "Amazing Grace" in about two dozen churches over the course of the campaign, including a lot of Southern Baptist churches.

In Phoenix I visited a large Baptist Church in an African American community with more than three thousand people in attendance. The bishop called me up to speak, and I told him I'd rather have the congregation join me in a song. I sang "Amazing Grace" with the full choir. It was funny because one of the bishop's congregants is an African American legislator in the Arizona House of Representatives. After I finished singing, the bishop went back to the podium, looked over to the legislator, and said, "Representative Campbell, where is your song?!"

I have a holiday CD that I made a few years ago. You'd get a kick out of it. I'm the third best—no, fifth best—Jewish holiday singer in the world. I'm behind Neil Diamond, Barry Manilow, Barbara Streisand, and one other person. I just don't know who it is, but I'm sure that fourth person is out there.

Advice

ONE OF THE GREATEST THINGS ABOUT running for office after being a small businessman, especially being in retail, is that I understand the importance of the customer and of every penny counting. I've put those practices into place on the Tucson City Council and in running for the U.S. Senate. Every person you meet in politics is a potential vote, just like every person you meet in business is a potential customer. But they have to see the value in you.

We have to work toward having business-friendly communities and elected officials and leadership in government that create less rules instead of more. Education is also extremely important. As a small businessman, the more you give back the better the schools and nonprofit organizations you will have, and the more the community will thrive and other businesses will want to locate there as well.

Building a coalition and creating consensus is not easy. But you start by having an open door on both sides. So often politicians don't take the time to listen to people they are afraid they might disagree with. Of course there will be differences, but it is really interesting to see when differing parties begin to talk with each other. It is a lot harder to hate someone if you can shake their hand.

The way I've run my campaigns and sought policies, like the rainwater-harvesting ordinance or opening schoolyards up to communities, has consistently reflected my long-term commitment to these values to listen to all sides and get everyone around the table working together. The best advice I would give for those thinking about running for office is remember that everyone has value. Everyone has insight and feedback.

In addition, remember the golden rule—treat others as you would want to be treated and do unto others as you would want them to do unto you. Period. If you live by that rule, and it's the way you treat your constituents and pursue your policymaking, your community is going to be a much better place.

There are times when I see young people who say they want to be like me. But I don't want young people to be like me. I want them to be better than me. Don't follow me, lead me. Be my partner in something. Let's do something great together. If you have something to add or a better idea, then share it with me. Because we are going to do much better working together.

Janet Chin, President
Garvey School District, California

History

MY FATHER'S FAMILY CAME TO THE United States in the 1920s, during the Chinese Exclusion Act [a federal law, enacted in 1882 and repealed in 1943 that made immigration from China illegal]. My grandfather came over when he was sixteen years old, under the name Chin Fook Sun, though his real name was Gong Yuen Tim. He worked for a Chinese laundry, and because he was the only employee with a driver's license, he drove the truck for the business. In the 1950s, he worked in agriculture and opened up a grocery store. He sometimes put in twenty-two-hour days.

My grandfather's greatest talent was numbers. He always knew at any given moment what the interest rates were and exactly how much money he had. In his later years, he was amazed that a fax machine could transmit the Monday morning receipts to him in San Francisco from my Aunt Mary in the store in Patterson, about one and a half hours away. But he never trusted a computer, and after he retired he still did figures by hand on his trusty calculator—the old-fashioned kind with a roll of paper. When my grandmother died, he counted each day after her death on that calculator—for exactly ten years.

What I loved most about my grandfather, who was seventy years old when I was born and lived past one hundred, was his discipline—not just for numbers, but for daily rituals. Each morning he put on his suit and tie, changed from his slippers to his dress shoes, attached his pedometer, and walked exactly five miles. He arrived every day at the same time at the community center of San Francisco's Fa Yuen Chinese Benevolent Association, which he helped to found and which still exists today. He taught me the importance of hard work as a means for success.

My mother's father was a colonel in the Chinese National Army, which was fighting the Communists in the 1940s. My mother was five years old when her father had to go to war. She and her mom had to run away, so that the Communists would not kidnap them. They were separated from her father for a very long time.

My mother started a Chinese Association here for people sharing her last name. Many people find that being connected globally through a family association with others outside of the native homeland is something very endearing and honorable, and it keeps growing in membership. It is a nice network, one of the oldest in California and fairly large, with many generations and branches in several cities.

My parents divorced when I was seven years old, and my father died when I was twelve. He was a very loving father, but he didn't really know how to father, and he spoiled his children. He made my mom promise that she would never get a job while we were in school, because he wanted to protect her, remembering how hard all of my aunts and uncles had worked in the grocery store, even at very young ages.

My mother has only an eleventh-grade education, but she is a very social person. She would often read something in the newspaper and automatically go and seek out the story to find out more about it. She's always had an affinity for the downtrodden, the impoverished, and people who come through great adversity. She feels that seeking justice for someone in pain is better than shedding a tear for them.

One day she read in the newspaper about an indigenous lady in Taiwan named Yang Mama. She was a farmer during an industrial boom, when Taiwanese people were moving from the countryside to work in factories in the larger cities. In 1986 my mother decided that, at ten years old, I was old enough to take my first trip, and she took my brother and me to Taiwan.

We stayed in an orphanage in the countryside for a week. There were many kids there, from babies to high school students. My brother and I immediately experienced a kind of culture shock. We were in a little village without running water, where the kids had to wash their clothes by hand. Even the dogs were orphans. We were seeing things we had never seen before.

The reason Yang Mama had made the newspaper was because after several years the Taiwanese government had learned about how she was transporting the kids to school. Separating the orphanage from the school was a river, which the children could not cross. Yang Mama would throw a rope across the river, put a child on her back, and use the rope as a guide as she walked across, so they would not wash away in the currents.

She would drop the children off one at a time and go back by that rope to get the next one. And she would do the same thing when they came home in the evening. When they learned about it, government officials immediately decided to construct a bridge and a building for the children, with a school, living quarters, and modern amenities such as electricity and running water.

One of the things I hold dear to my heart is a story about a little boy, two years old at most, who came up to me and grabbed onto my leg. I was really proud of this yellow-and-white dress I was wearing that day. The little boy was dirty, and it looked like he had been eating a mango, and some of it was caked on the dirt. I just remember him being incredibly sticky and grimy, and he had his legs wrapped around mine, and I tried so hard to peel him off of me, but I did not want to touch him. I remember that my mom shot me the Look—you know, like in the movies when something happens and there is this zoom into the headshot. I felt like she flew right up to me and said, "Don't you dare do that. Don't you know this boy does not have a mother?"

I could never forget that image of "children hanging on to each other because they have no one else to hold on to." The older ones take care of the younger ones, and the younger ones take care of the even younger ones. In essence, they are a family.

From then on, it was my dream to have my own youth organization. I didn't necessarily think it was going to be an orphanage, but I was constantly thinking about how guilty I felt about that moment and how, even at age ten, I should have understood that children without parents need each other and need a community.

At seventeen, I joined the Army National Guard through the early-entry program. My mother had to sign me in, and she was reluctant at first, asking if I was sure this was what I wanted to do. Of course that was what I wanted to do, because my family did not have money to pay for a college education. And I always knew that my father had enlisted at the age of seventeen for the Korean War. I remember him saying it was the best time of his life.

My father was given a Purple Heart because he saved someone's life in battle. It wasn't so much the glory I wanted, but enlisting seemed like the honorable thing to do. I was the first of my father's children to join the Army and follow in his footsteps in some way. He had joined the Army partly because he was running away, and in some ways I was running away too, because I didn't want to live where I grew up for my entire life.

I remember the brief moment of leaving my mother when I headed out for training. You know Chinese people don't hug, and it was a clean departure, and I was on the journey. I served a year and a half in the National Guard, and I learned so much, in the South especially. I grew as a person through the experience.

I was part of Operation Uphold Democracy. During that time, President Aristide of Haiti was being overthrown by guerrilla fighters. The Marines, Army, and Navy were cooperating with one another in very hazardous conditions. I was a top-secret communications specialist, serving in a secluded area surrounded by metal wiring and guarded twenty-four hours a day, part of a satellite communications unit that routed messages all over the world.

Throughout my Army experience, I was always a "youth person." I volunteered for all kinds of events for children and organized youth festivals. I've always had an affinity for children, and I appreciate the ways I've been able to impact their lives.

We were in the poorest country in the world. I remember this little girl named Emma, who was about nine or ten years old. She was very small. I worked the night shift, and I remember her coming by each day in the early morning when I was getting off my shift. I'm sure she'd never seen anyone like me before, an Asian American soldier. I guess she thought I was interesting, and of course I thought she was interesting, too.

In my mom's stories of wartime from her childhood, she remembers soldiers giving her candy, gum, and other things she had never seen before, and sometimes telling her stories while she sat on their laps. I gave candy and gum and coloring books to Emma, which I got from care packages. I would give her whatever I could find. She came every single morning, when I was trying to go to bed after being up all night. She would stand at the fence outside our compound and yell, "Chin-Chin."

Sometimes she got inside, maybe with a relative the Army had hired to do cleaning. I didn't really know who she was, and I didn't speak Creole to be able to find out. But we tried to communicate through charades. Then, suddenly, right before we were to leave, she disappeared and I didn't see her again.

Politics

EVER SINCE MY TIME IN HAITI, Emma has always been with me. She was really bold coming into the compound and interacting with someone she had never seen before. I felt like there was a special connection between her and me. After I got home, I helped to start a Youth Foundation, including a program for girls called EMA, which stands for Etiquette and Manners Academy. I always tell the girls within our program about Emma.

My colleagues and I chartered the Youth Foundation in my hometown. It began as primarily an organization helping young people to do service-oriented projects and creative volunteering in their communities. From the very beginning, we wanted our Youth Board to make the decisions and guide everything we did. The board is comprised of seven members, and they come up with the goals, agendas, and decisions about what we work on and fund.

About a year into it, we began to realize how much of the foundation work was about education. That's where the students are, and that's where they need the most help. We switched gears to become primarily an education charity.

Around this time, in 2007, I decided to run for the School Board. At the time our community was changing, and I believed it was ready to move forward with a grassroots campaign for community building. I was president of the PTA, the English Language Learners Council, and a School Site Council. I felt that the missing piece for most students was parent and family engagement, which was the case mostly because most parents and families are working these days.

Campaigning

THE KEY ISSUE IN MY PLATFORM was parental involvement, which I became well known for. We all know that teachers and principals respond to children whose parents are paying attention, and kids feel more special when their parents are involved. The other focus of my campaign was community involvement, with an emphasis on collaboration. I can't do everything, and neither can others, but we can work together and build community.

At almost every door on which I knocked, the same motivations and key concerns emerged from the parents. Most talked about wanting after-school programs for their children. Our Youth Foundation had already started after-school programs, and people knew that I was a huge advocate for such programs, which helped me in the campaign. I was about a hundred votes away from being the top vote getter in a two-seat race.

The Garvey School District is the second oldest in Los Angeles County, which has more than two hundred districts. We have eleven schools, running from kindergarten through eighth grade. We have a technical school and a performing-arts school, but no high school. We've had to close two schools in the past three years. There are many gaps in the school district, and we're trying to fill them.

We also have a bilingual school, because our community has many immigrants. Eight languages are spoken by our students, primarily Chinese, Vietnamese, English, and Spanish. Fifty-three percent of our students are Asian, and 46 percent are Latino. Eighty-seven percent get free or reduced-cost lunches. We have received awards for distinguished achievement. We are a leader among schools connected to Stephen Covey's "Seven Habits of Highly Successful Students," which are part of our curriculum.

The Youth Foundation has been a very important tool for us to collaborate with many nonprofits in our community. We have students who organize fundraisers to raise money for our school district. Last summer they raised $1,500. They know these institutions are struggling, and they want to be a part of helping them. It's given them a platform for speaking out, and that is really the premise of the Youth Foundation: empowering kids.

The foundation has three divisions: Afterschool Academics, Youth Leadership Academy, and Youth Issues, which is a college-based data collection component. We're moving toward being a neighborhood resource center, serving about four hundred students a year. A lot of our assistants come from the CalWorks program, which is for parents transitioning into industries through job rehabilitation and training. They are either single parents or older siblings who are taking care of younger children and who can't go to school because they have to work.

I believe the kids respect me. Being able to speak with them on their level is crucial. So many children suffer neglect and abuse and have to go through so many sacrifices because the adults around them are unable to take care of them or give them opportunities. Their stories bring me to tears. And they become part of my life. Knowing their trials and hardships helps me to go on, with a profound commitment to changing things.

Maybe I have an old soul, but young people are craving for someone that looks like them and thinks like them and says to them, "You can do this." As young kids and teenagers, they're often told what not to do, and there's not a lot of permission given to explore and question. Someone has to be the one, and you can be that role model that gives them that permission. They need to see adults out there speaking on the issues, whether it's on the environment or immigration or our need to be good neighbors and increase public safety.

Our School Board members each have their own agendas, and the ways we go about things and prioritize may be different. But they all care about the students and achievement and having a cohesive staff. I've been the School Board president for about seven months now, and it has been sometimes painful and at other times proud.

As a School Board member, I was a sponge, observing and listening. I didn't have the gavel in my hand, and it was a nice opportunity. Now that I'm president, everything has to go through me. Like a mayor, I'm a symbol, shaking hands and doing speeches, and I also put together our agendas and steer the process. It's humbling to know that I'm actually steering and guiding the lives of the children in my district.

At times I question the direction of the board. Our agenda right now is hiring a new superintendent, which is critical to our future. We're also focusing on teacher evaluations, pushing the unions on this issue. We have a $20 million contract for green technology, which will change how we do business in the next twenty years.

I'm making all these decisions knowing that I won't be here in ten years, that I won't be a board member who stays on for twenty or thirty years. The decisions I make will fall into someone else's lap. Contracts we implement will be here long after I'm gone. Even though I serve a small school district, I take seriously being the leader of the vision.

Advice

MANY CITIZENS SIMPLY WANT TO GET their say. My day job is with the Social Security Administration. We serve skid row, and many of our clients have mental issues and great needs. They just want to be heard, too. They want to know that we care that they're still alive.

Sometimes I can get bogged down in routines and responsibilities. But the most important thing is to say to my constituents, "I hear you. How can I help?" You can make a situation go sour or get better. It's critical to know the situations you're walking into, scope them out, stay calm, and listen.

Building a gym or a skyscraper is easier than tearing down an ego. If I become selfish, I'll be ruined. Our communities need people who can build partnerships. I may not like you, but I can work with you and say good things about you in the public arena. The best word I ever got was from Judy Chu, who is my representative in Congress: "No friends are permanent, and no enemies are permanent."

The best advice I can think to give to young people considering running for public office is just do it. I'm about action, so I'd say do it. We are not doing justice to our children, and we need people in public office who are willing to walk a fine line, instead of taking detours.

I encourage young people to get involved in the political process. Many would love to intern with campaigns, and I tell this to folks in the YEO [Young Elected Officials] network. A lot of young elected officials don't have staff, unless they're in the larger cities, and interns can help to get so much done, returning phone calls, raising money, writing thank-you notes. And this helps to bring along younger people who are interested in politics and builds their resumes.

I think it is crucial for every elected official always to be looking for the next person to take his or her place. As soon as you're elected, you should be looking and nurturing future leaders. Much of the power within politics is helping to bring of age and train younger people to carry on your mission. Set goals, give them tools, and keep pushing.

There are times when I see young people who say they want to be like me. But I don't want young people to be like me. I want them to be better than me. Don't follow me; lead me. Be my partner in something. Let's do something great together. If you have something to add, or a better idea, then share it with me. Because we are going to do much better working together than if I ordered you around, with you waiting for me to think for you, or to give you instructions. If you can do things better, then by all means lead.

My leadership in public service and ministry doesn't just take me to the edge. We get taken over the edge and awakened at ever deepening levels, so that we can be with people in need—to serve and to help.

Rev. Dr. Simeon Queen
City Council, Prairie View, Texas

History

I WAS RAISED ON CONSERVATIVE VALUES. My parents came out of a strict Pentecostal background, and both are pastors and part of the evangelical movement. My dad was the first African American pastor at the Church on the Rock—one of the first and largest mega-churches in the country. That nondenominational congregation exposed me to a mixture of influences and experiences. When I was young, I felt like fear and love were fighting each other. I got to see the best of both sides, so to speak, of what God had to offer and what the world had to offer. Half of my family members were drug lords, and the other half were ministers. I felt I had to choose between two distinct roads.

When I was eight years old, I stood up and recited several pieces of scripture in church. Before I turned eleven, I had read through the Bible twice. I have always considered the Word of God to be my key of faith, and it became life to me. I gave away all my toys and studied all the time. I also loved singing Gregorian chant. I knew I was "different."

At the age of eleven, I became a minister, preaching the Word of God. I was learning everything that preachers normally learn, but not within the context of the African American church. The Church on the Rock was 99 percent white. I took spiritual development classes and studied hermeneutics. The program took seven years to complete, and I was the only child in all those classes.

Politics

I attended Prairie View A&M University. It was founded at the same time as Texas A&M, and the two institutions are branches of the same tree. At their founding, former President of the Confederate States Jefferson Davis was offered the presidency of both. He respectfully recommended that a "colored man," W. L. Minor, a citizen of Mississippi, serve as Prairie View's "principal." He didn't feel that the African American institution deserved a president.

That discrimination continued for a long time. Prairie View A&M had five principals before it had a president. Until 1956 African American students from the area could go nowhere but Prairie View, and small towns all over Texas sent their best. Recent commencement speakers at the 8,600-student university have included Rick Perry and both President Bushes. During the university's 131-year history, no graduate has ever served on the university system's Board of Regents that makes decisions impacting both institutions, and the student body has no say in policy.

While I was attending the university, county law enforcement officers began targeting Prairie View students, issuing speeding tickets to students who weren't speeding. I decided it was time to try to make a difference, so I jumped in. I felt there was a need for representation of the minority community at the county level, and I ran for Justice of the Peace in 2001 at the age of twenty-one. The only qualifications for the office, which oversaw traffic tickets and other misdemeanors, were being at least eighteen years old and being registered with the Selective Service. I ran as a write-in candidate and lost terribly.

In 2003 I ran for county commissioner. I won the Republican primary against another candidate. I've never believed in the whole platform of either the Republican or Democrat Party; I was just following where my passion led. Lots of my family members were Republicans along with a white man who was an elder in our church. He was a stern Republican and role model early in my life. Even to this day, he is still like a second father to me.

Primary Day fell during spring break, and most students were gone, which made it hard for me to get the votes. But I worked hard, sponsoring barbecues and sending out supporter-donated limousines for transportation to the polls. In a strongly Democratic precinct, I got the most votes ever recorded for a Republican. I lost to the Democrat, an older man, in a contentious general election. He had also spread a lot of misinformation about me and took a sample ballot I had produced for students and redesigned it to his advantage.

My whole ethos began to change when I started working with homeless people at St. John's United Methodist Church in Houston in 2005. St. John's has more than thirteen thousand congregants, and three thousand are either homeless or formerly homeless. We serve 144,000 meals every year and run an emergency shelter, as well as offer employment and housing services, support groups, and life skills and anger management training. Our culinary arts program trains homeless people to be cooks and caterers, and Art Project Houston is an entrepreneurial project for homeless brothers and sisters who have skills in painting, sculpting, or photography, which raises money for them as well as the shelter.

At St. John's I began to understand the systemic dynamics of homelessness. Some people who get up for work every morning come back to the shelter at night, because they don't earn enough money to afford housing. Others struggle with mental illnesses or felony convictions that make them unemployable. More and more, we see young people on the run and families that lost their homes when they lost their jobs.

As the need is getting greater, the resources are shrinking. The state recently cut our funding by $2.4 million. We've been forced to scale back our services, and we had to lay off thirty of our thirty-five workers. We've had to move from being an employee-based to a volunteer-based organization, which has been very difficult.

Homeless people need us. When I started at St. John's, I called on a number of my Republican friends. They helped, not because of their party affiliation but because they knew me. That's when I started praying and asking for enlightenment about my politics.

I switched to the Democratic Party. Staying Republican would have been the more reasonable choice, because I was up for an appointment by the governor, and I had created a base of support. But God laid it on my heart to switch, and I believe that is what God wanted for me. I'm happy with it.

Campaigning

DURING MY FIRST CAMPAIGN FOR JUSTICE of the Peace, I was predicted to win, even though I was really "green." I had no idea what I was doing; I just wanted to help my community. I spent $5,000 in savings and bought all the yard signs I could afford. I had at least three hundred.

The guy I ran against removed more than half my signs. People actually had pictures of him stealing them from yards. I decided not to use those pictures against him. I said things like, "The Lord is going to fight my battles!" My opponent won.

At the end of the race, he walked over and said, "Reverend Queen, I want you to know it wasn't really personal. Man, I've been out of work for three years. I have a wife and kids, and I really needed this job." He'd run and lost three or four times before. "I do apologize for stealing your signs."

He continued, "I can honestly say you ran a race with integrity, but I had to do what I had to do to win. I want to tell you, no matter how many great values or ideas about policy you have or how you want to make change, if you don't win, no one will ever know." That was eye-opening. Someone can have the greatest values and ideas and political strategy, but the point is, if you don't win, no one will be helped.

But winning can't be everything. I've found that the only thing that transcends politics is love. I think most politicians want to create that in campaigns, but at times I believe they only put up a good front as to what it means to love everyone. They treat people well only because each person represents a vote. The main motivation is self-interest. When your campaign platform is about winning, votes can very easily be the lens through which you see the world and your political success.

A lot of people just do not want to operate in love. It is easier to operate out of fear. True love stretches you from that place you want to be, to the place where God wants you to be. It's the only thing I've seen that has trumped the political system. It is a different kind of freedom to be able to love everybody, to be with people from different backgrounds in love.

When I ran for county commissioner the first time, I wrote an article introducing myself to the community and published it in the local newspaper with my picture. At the last debate, a white couple came up and told me they had read the article. The man said, "I honestly thought I'd never vote for a black man. But for the first time ever, we are going to vote for a black man."

I was floored by his comments, but at the same time I was honored. It showed me that things are not too far gone. I mean, I had to fight as a student to get Colored signs taken down at the County Courthouse. They were not very visible, but they were still there.

A few years later, I got a lot of the Caucasian votes when I ran for county commissioner, even in the more conservative rural areas, because I knocked on people's doors. When I got elected in 2005 to the Prairie View City Council, I won by eleven votes. In 2007 I won by more than a hundred votes, among 450 cast.

Prairie View was built on an old slave plantation. It's in the area of the country that was the last to accept the Emancipation Proclamation. Some people consider Prairie View, with its significant civil rights history, the bellwether of progress, or lack of it, for African Americans in Texas.

The economic climate and social fabric still festers with broken fragments like the "Prairie View Plantation" of yesterday. During slavery, African Americans worked hard and made lots of other people rich. When slavery ended, new mechanisms were put in place to make money off the same people and their descendants. Millions of dollars flow through Prairie View to the outskirts of the city but do not stay in the community.

When you look at resource availability in the county—whether for education, economic development, or infrastructure—the allocation is inherently unequal. Even the mail service for our city has been discriminatory. The U.S. Postal Service is supposed to guarantee a free option for postal delivery. We have no home delivery in Prairie View, and for sixty years residents have been paying for their Post Office boxes.

The most recent fight is over equality in schools. African American kids get used books and a school built in the 1950s that lacks air conditioning.

The county just floated a $49 million bond, and only $200,000 was designated for the Prairie View School. The rest went to build two new elementary schools in an upscale development and a brand-new, $18 million football stadium. I've been involved with colleagues, making news with lots of press conferences about the inequity.

Prairie View has a five-member City Council and a $3 million annual budget. My first year on council, we passed our first bond for building a City Hall, improving infrastructure, paving streets, and bringing our water system up to par. For the first time ever, Prairie View has a City Hall. Efficiency, professionalism, and empowerment of community members are at an all-time high. The veil is lifting.

Advice

"INTEGRITY RULES" IS THE BEST POLITICAL advice I've gotten. A candidate in a Congressional race once tried to buy me for $100,000. Claiming that it was God's will for him to win the election, he tried to get me to put his name on a sample ballot I was creating. I think refusing him was the best thing I ever did politically, because it rang across the county that I could not be bought.

It's hard as a young politician not to get caught up in the politics. In this day and age, people understand that movements are created by young people. When they see a young person who is an empowering leader and interested in politics, they will try to use him or her until they can't use that person anymore. It is important for young leaders to be able to stand on their own two feet and say clearly, "I can't be bought."

My advice to young candidates is stay focused and keep your values. And don't be afraid to run. It's never too early to make effective change. Also, don't be afraid to say the critical things that would help the community instead of helping yourself. I got into politics for the people, not what I could get for myself.

I've discovered that wisdom comes at times through failure. In terms of getting my yard signs stolen, I guess the Lord had to show me something. I've learned that even though something might be a good idea, that doesn't mean it's a God idea.

I would say that God is not a Republican or a Democrat. I know, because I've been both. The experience of being a Republican most of my life and a Democrat in the latter part has shown me that, if I talk to Democrats out of love, they receive it. If I talk to Republicans out of love, they receive it as well.

But if I talk out of fear as a Republican about Democrats, or as a Democrat about Republicans, they receive that, too. In politics people tend to feed off of fear, which is the total opposite of love. Love is often the difference between hostility and competitiveness or partnership and cooperation.

In terms of my religious faith, early on I felt like I had to sacrifice everything to show God that I loved Him. In reality I never actually sacrificed anything. Most of the things I did, I did because I wanted to be associated with a "good boy" box. That box was formulated and created by other people's opinions based on an old system of what a good Christian or minister was supposed to be.

I would say now that I feel like I am more centered in the main tenets of God's truth. It's a truth rooted in transparency, which is empowering. When God puts you in a place where you more fully understand your own vulnerabilities and capabilities, you go on living in the way that He created you and wants you to live.

I recently had a compelling vision come to me. In the vision I was on top of a cliff with a lot of Christians. We heard a great roaring sound that was disorienting. Everybody looked around, saying, "We don't see anything."

God told me to walk over to the edge of the cliff. Letting go of my fear and anxiety, I walked to the edge and looked over. I was in awe as I saw a sea of people. I turned to those beside me on the cliff and said, "Hey, come help me! I see all these people below in need."

They looked at me incredulously, saying, "No, you're too close to the edge, and you may fall."

And I said, "How can we help these people?" God led me to try to pull up one person at a time. So I started pulling them up, and before I knew it, there was a whole group of people from the cliff helping me pull the others up. They too had let go of their fear, or their socialization, or their comfort.

But it did not happen immediately. In order to help those people in need, it was absolutely necessary to go to the edge to see their eyes, their faces, and what they were going through—to break out of our comfort zone. In essence, we had to see life as they were seeing it, to impact and be impacted by them and to have the courage to act.

In the end, my leadership in public service and ministry doesn't just take me to the edge. We get taken over the edge and awakened at ever deepening levels so that we can be with those people in need—to serve and to help.

I find that I'm at my best when I can love many people, regardless of their background or belief. I'm not separating gays from straights, or being restricted by political background, or putting "enemies" in boxes, so to speak. When one is able to embody that kind of leadership, it brings about a whole different feel as to who a leader is and how a leader acts. Once that happens, I find myself in situations where the reality I'm in at the moment takes me to places I'd never expect. Or I'm inspired in ways that inform my actions in unlikely ways.

Jesus came to give us life, and a life lived abundantly. He came teaching the kingdom of God and said, "Greater works shall you do." But we focus a lot of times on just saying we are Christians instead of trying to figure out what God is calling us to do. Sometimes people believe that God just wants us to live a good life, but that usually leaves you outside of that place on the edge that would deepen and enrich your faith journey.

My book is called *The Church or the Club: Who Is Winning?* It shows how many people would rather be sitting in Starbucks or playing at the country club or shopping at Walmart than being in church. Why is that? It's probably because the church is not giving out that love that kills people's fear.

The book provides a framework for the prism through which we see. If the club is winning, you'll see the Gospel in the world out of the club's eyes. And if the kingdom is winning, you'll see politics and people in the kingdom's eyes.

My experience of coming from a very conservative background in my religious faith and then later experiencing a very liberal Christian environment has led me to believe in the unconditional nature of God's love. It is that unconditional love that transcends differences and can bring all things into alignment.

Jesus spent his early years in the temple, gaining a formal understanding of religion. In his later years, he was on the highways and byways, surrounding himself with people considered not so favorable, learning a different kind of love. From a kingdom perspective, he found a component of love in both.

I'm in training to be a spiritual director for the United Methodist Church. When I'm through, I'll be the youngest spiritual director in the denomination and the only African American male. In the process,

I've learned to address my own fears and prejudices and examine my foundational truths.

As a child, I was taught particular things about other faiths. One day at St. John's, I was getting basic intake information from a few homeless men. One claimed to be a Moor, another Muslim, and two others confessed to being atheists. I had a good conversation with each one of them. As we got to know each other, I could look past their circumstances and see a piece of God's love in each one of them. And when I showed the love of God in me to them, I believe they were receptive as well.

At St. John's, we have several Muslim congregations that come by every three or four months. The Imam brings the members of his mosque to observe the true love of Jesus that they read about in the Quran. Once or twice a month, we have Buddhists come to serve our homeless sisters and brothers and encourage them in love. They cook food at their temple and bring it over, and we have a wonderful time.

I've learned that if we don't take the time to study Americans at their weakest points, we're not doing a very consistent job of building prosperity for all. A homeless brother or sister is almost always at his or her weakest point. Homeless people are vulnerable and leaning on someone else to help them. For us not to study what brought them to that place, and for us not to search our hearts and our policies and try to change this system, is, I believe, irresponsible.

What is really important about my work with the homeless is that it makes me a more compassionate public servant. I say that as someone who is going through a deeper and deeper conversion in my work. Public servants tend to get caught up in our own world. Every day I am reminded of just how fortunate I am, and where I or my family could be. It is sobering, humbling, and empowering, all at the same time.

As a mother raising young children in the community that I grew up in, I didn't want to see the violence of gangs in Lennox's next generation. A lot of my peers dropped out of school and society, and many were killed by that violence. Sometimes I feel that we're a lost generation. Education I believe is the ultimate equalizer, the key to a different future.

Marisol Cruz
School Board, Lennox, California

History

WHEN I WAS A BABY, MY father could not find a job where we lived in Jalisco, Mexico. He wanted to provide for his young family, so we migrated within Mexico to a city. He worked for a short time, but then that job fell through. So he came to the United States to make a better life for his family, and my mother soon joined him.

When I was three months of age, my older brother and I came here. My mother didn't know at the time that she was pregnant with my little brother. It was scary, from what my mom tells me, putting her children in the hands of complete strangers—*los coyotes*, the smugglers who helped us cross the border—hoping and trusting that they would return us safe and sound after crossing. Fortunately, we made it, and reunited with my parents.

After high school, I decided to go to college, because I knew that I did not want to work from sunrise to sunset like my parents do. I attended El Camino Community College. I was twenty-one years old, separated from my husband, and a single mother of two. I later transferred to California State University at Long Beach and received a degree in psychology, with a concentration in women's studies.

In college I awoke to a bigger reality and began to see how society is arranged. There are people in power; there's a system in place, and things don't just happen by accident. There is a reason why we live in a little barrio, a community one mile square that is almost entirely Latino. Many of us in Lennox live in poverty amid gang violence and drugs and all the stereotypical assumptions. That is our reality.

I woke up to the reality of politics and how things work. I began to understand how "the personal is political, and the political is personal." I began to see how the system is set up for us to fail. That is what fueled my passion. And that is what got me into activism.

Politics

WHEN I WAS TWENTY-FIVE AND enrolling my older son in kindergarten, I found out that the Lennox School Board had decided to do away with classes in Spanish. In a community that is 98 percent Latino, they were taking away the home language, which is like taking away our identity. At the same time, they had decided to do away with immersion programs that would have helped students to learn English. I was outraged.

A group of parents and teachers organized *Padres Unidos de Lennox*— Parents United of Lennox. They were looking for a candidate to run for the School Board. I was still a single mother trying to get through college, which was difficult enough. But I felt such anger at the injustice of the board's acts that I told the grassroots organization that if they couldn't find anyone else, I would be interested in running. Shortly thereafter, they interviewed me; we found we had a lot in common, and I became a candidate.

I believe that things happen for a reason, and the timing of it all was mind boggling. Sometimes I feel like I'm living in a constant state of miracles. You wake up to a world of beauty and love, but when you look more closely you see people living in misery and pain, held there by a system that's in place, and you know you need to do something about it.

I wanted to make a difference. As a mother raising young children in the community that I grew up in, I didn't want to see the violence of gangs in Lennox's next generation. A lot of my peers dropped out of school and society, and many were killed by that violence. Sometimes I feel that we're a lost generation. Education, I believe, is the ultimate equalizer, the key to a different future.

Campaigning

THE MEMBERS OF PADRES UNIDOS HAD a lot of social capital between them. They found a campaign manager to work for free. In the beginning, I didn't know what I was doing, so I did a lot of learning. We all learned together as a group, and the manager showed us how to run a campaign.

I did not run a typical campaign. I didn't know anything about fundraising. I walked around with my two boys, then ages four and five, to local businesses. I had no pamphlets, no literature. It was just me and my kids walking around, asking for contributions. And I think the businesses were like, what is this crazy lady doing here?

Trying to raise money for the race was hard, because four years ago people had no idea what the School Board was or what those who served on it did. I'd get a five-dollar contribution here and there. I called my family and they helped. I raised about four hundred dollars. I look back now and think, what the hell *was* I doing!

Four people were running for three seats. A teachers' aide in a neighboring school and I ran as a slate, with the endorsements of the Lennox Teachers Association, the local teachers' union, and the local newspaper. The only incumbent lost, and the three candidates with no political experience won. With 1,300 votes, I was the top vote getter and was elected to a four-year term.

I initially felt isolated. Historically, the School Board was a rubber-stamping board. I'm a person who questions things a lot. The slate we had put together and an alliance we built with another candidate fell apart, further isolating me.

At the beginning, I normally got outvoted four to one. For example, I wanted to build a task force to look into the English learners' program and a committee to explore bilingual education and English immersion. While my supporters in the community were cheering me on, I found myself being outvoted four to one on the board—on these and many other issues.

One of the first things I needed to understand in my transition to elected office was that we needed a majority—at least three votes—to pass anything. I guess now I'm a politician, since I relate differently to my colleagues on the board. I learned very quickly not to be aggressive, because people may be scared off. Some are afraid of change and make things difficult.

After I served two years on the board, two seats were up for election. So we learned how to run a campaign as progressives in our district, and we won the two seats. Now I'm usually in a three to two majority on votes.

When I moved into the majority, we had to make a lot of decisions quickly, and some were very difficult. There were human resource issues. The most challenging was removing a principal from an elementary school, for which we got some backlash. I knew that we did the right thing, but there were things we knew that we couldn't disclose, and the management of the issue was a disaster. Because of that, we were put in a position where people didn't understand what we were doing, and some were upset.

We need the appropriate framework, so that mismanagement of such decisions doesn't cause them to blow up in our faces. As a result of that issue, we're working on a clear vision and a strategic plan to build a bridge between the school district and the Lennox community. We want parents to be more involved in the decision-making process, to be educated to think for themselves and not be manipulated by others' interests. We want more avenues of feedback and communication. Accountability is also an important attribute in the process, so that we can rest assured that there are checks and balances in our system. It can be really frustrating in a culture where people are used to giving up their power and rights.

Lennox is right next to Los Angeles, and we are the gatekeepers to LAX Airport. People fly over us and drive around us all the time, creating a lot of pollution. Lennox residents, like my parents, have typically been the workforce at the airport, in the hotels, and in other parts of the service industry.

Most people are working parents, who don't get the pay and benefits, as well as the respect and dignity they deserve. Many mothers and fathers have to work two or three jobs, with children left at home fending for themselves. They are left in a neighborhood with peer pressure and gangs, and the cycle within the community starts all over again.

In 2006 we organized three hundred people to participate in civil disobedience. We had tried to do it the nice way, expressing our concerns to employers about low pay and lack of respect, but with corporations that doesn't really work. I was arrested with neighbors and parents of children in the Lennox School District during a sit-in on Century Boulevard. We closed down the street from the Westin Hotel to the Hilton.

Things have definitely changed with the School Board. We have revolutionized the community and the school system. It's no longer true, as it was four years ago, that people don't know who we are or what we do. After a lot of work and effort, we now have a dual English-Spanish immersion program, which is quite an accomplishment. We've made so many changes so rapidly, people are paying attention.

But our families and community are still struggling. When the mortgage crisis hit, people began losing their homes. Now sometimes you see two or three families living in one house, because people are just trying to survive, and rental prices are very expensive. People who have the means are converting garages and adding rooms to make more space.

The breakdown of families is propelling young people into gangs. A strong family is built on jobs and education. It's my dream to make that happen for everyone in Lennox. I want to give the power with which we've been entrusted back to the people, to organize people in the community to take a leadership role. *Mas que nada.* More than anything.

If you think about what's happened on the School Board, we've been very successful. But I certainly haven't benefited personally from public service. I'm still living in my parents' house, making barely enough to pay rent and struggling to buy my kids shoes. If I want to make things happen for me financially, I have to steer away from activism and organizing.

But I want to do all that I can to make things happen for my community, while I'm entrusted with power to be a vehicle for change. If I'm sacrificing and giving myself up for the community for four or eight years, so that things will be better for my boys and their generation, I'm okay with that. Selfless acts for others are beautiful.

Advice

I believe in me. Is that political advice? And having a strong belief in others and in what you're doing is important. Other people believed in me before I believed in myself. I just knew I wanted to help people. They saw something in me, and through the political process, I found myself. So now I too believe in me and in what I'm doing, and I'm standing strong on that rock.

Election night was a "school night," of course. I had had a test in class that day, and I was so nervous I couldn't stand it. I voted early that morning. Since I had just turned eighteen, it was my first election, and it was cool that the first time I could vote I could vote for myself.

Sara Humm
City Commissioner
Ottawa, Kansas

History

NO ONE IN MY FAMILY IS involved with politics. Except my grandpa, who was the mayor of his very small town—but that was because no one else was interested. All four years of high school I ran for student body representative, and I lost every time.

During my junior and senior years, I was part of my city's Youth in Government program at Ottawa High School, which was featured by the National League of Cities and Municipalities as an outstanding model. I spent a year and a half attending city meetings and learning what was going on with local government. Every year the group does a project to help the community as a whole. We decided to take on the task of supporting an effort to pass a smoking ban—a "clean air ordinance"—in Ottawa. In previous years, other groups made several attempts to get the ban passed, all of which failed.

One day after school, I was sitting in front of the TV watching our government access channel. You'd be surprised how many people watch that channel. There was an advertisement about signing up for elections to run for City Commission. I thought to myself, I might want to do that.

I called my mom and said, "Mom, I have something to tell you."

She was like, "Okay?"

So I told her, "I think I want to run for City Commission."

And she said, "Well, you know, I'm not surprised."

I was seventeen years old. I wasn't sure how it would work, because the election was in April and my birthday is in February. I went and talked to some people at City Hall who knew me from the Youth in Government program. They told me that I had to be eighteen by the cut-off date for the primary election on February 27th. My birthday is February 24th. I made the cut-off by three days.

Politics

MY DAD DIED FROM CANCER IN September, a few months before I decided to run. I realized from that experience that it's possible to get through very difficult things and that life goes on. I regret that my dad passed away before he knew I was going to run and that he wasn't there to celebrate my win.

My family has been in Ottawa, a community with thirteen thousand residents, for more than thirty years. I believe lots of people were surprised that I decided to run. It was a huge step for me, and I knew I was going to have a tough time.

Five people, including three incumbents, were running for three positions. The top two vote getters would serve four-year terms, with the third getting a two-year term. I had a lot of work to do, and I wasn't sure how it was all going to get done. But I was willing to take on the challenge.

Campaigning

CANDIDATE YARD SIGNS IN OTTAWA HAD always been red, white, and blue, designed to look patriotic. I decided to be more hip, because I was eighteen. My yard signs were white and teal, and the pens I handed out were purple and teal. My fliers were bright orange. I went with a New Age style and colors that would grab attention and stand out a little more. It really worked.

I had a lot of help from family and friends. My high school friends were involved, because my campaign was the most exciting thing happening to them. We went door to door on weekends. A lot of people were impressed that I was knocking on doors and making that commitment. I got a lot of votes just by being seen and being willing to go out and tell people what I was about.

I knew that I was young, and I knew a lot of people were skeptical of young people, because some think young people are inexperienced and don't know what's going on in the community. But I believe that's not true. I knew more about the community than some of the candidates, and knew a different part of the community from others, including commissioners who have served a long time. But running against three older, more experienced incumbents and participating in candidate forums with them was incredibly intimidating.

I think a lot of people were initially skeptical about me, believing that I didn't have enough experience. But once I explained my involvement in Youth in Government for two years, and my regular attendance at City Commission meetings, voters saw that I knew the needs in the community and understood the lingo.

I used my age to my advantage. Instead of identifying myself as "young," I used the slogan "Fresh voice and new opinions." Everyone on the commission had been there for several years. Some of them have children and even grandchildren my age. I saw my campaign as an opportunity to show a different aspect, from the younger side of the community.

A lot of the youth in our community were discouraged, because they felt their voices were not being heard. They would say that there's nothing for them to do downtown and nothing being done about it. Students were excited about my campaign, because they saw someone running who could relate to them. And that gave encouragement to other people who felt they didn't have a voice.

I came in a solid second. The two others who were elected were both incumbents. The candidate who came in fifth had served on the commission for sixteen years and had played a prominent role in starting the Youth in Government program. I felt a little bad about beating the man who essentially got me started in politics through the program he helped create. But I realized that he and his colleagues created it for a reason. And, obviously, it worked!

Election night was a "school night," of course. I had had a test in class that day, and I was so nervous I couldn't stand it. I voted early that morning. Since I had just turned eighteen, it was my first election, and it was cool that the first time I could vote I could vote for myself. My mom and I went to vote together, and then I had to sit through school the whole day, which felt brutal. All I wanted was for it to be night, so I could find out if I'd won or not.

That night we had a get-together at my house with friends and family. My government teacher came and that was great, because she was a huge encouragement and mentor to me. People came over and we had snacks, and then we went to the courthouse to watch the results come in.

I loved that. Each time a precinct reported in, the staff wrote the results on a white board, then printed out the numbers and gave a copy to each candidate. It was a very fun and exciting evening. I was in the top two or three the entire time.

I got the word that I had come in second a while before the County Clerk came in and made it official. There was lots of excitement and lots of hugs. And then the newspaper and radio interviews came. At barely eighteen years old, I was the youngest person in the nation elected to public office.

The next day at school, the principal came onto the loudspeaker and announced the win. It was an amazing moment. I definitely had to start thinking more about who I was hanging around with and how I spent my time. It was important to me to represent myself and the city well.

Once I won, the shock factor set in. I had confidence in myself, but I knew I had lots of work to do. It was an adjustment, because I had to fit in six commission meetings a month with school, homework, my extracurricular activities, and my job. I was a waitress at Applebee's, which was beneficial, because people saw me as down to earth. I'm a regular person, who was making $2.13 an hour plus what I could get in tips.

There's a sixty-year difference between the oldest member of the commission and me. I feel very fortunate, because I've heard so many horror stories from other young elected officials about not getting along with their fellow officials. There have been times we've disagreed, but we are still able to work together and respect each other at the end of the day.

After I was elected, we got the clean-air ordinance passed. That was a cool moment for me. It was great to see it made law and have such an impact, which I'd had a hand in starting and voted for.

The toughest vote I faced was on rezoning an area from residential to commercial. I was torn about it. To pass, a supermajority—four members—of the Commission had to vote for it. One had already voted against it, and I was the second-to-last vote. My no vote defeated it. I beat myself up a little, but at the end of the day I believed I'd done the right thing for the betterment of the community.

After the meeting, my mom asked me, "Did you vote from your heart?"

I said yes. She responded, that was all I could do. What I took away from that was, people can try to persuade you so many different ways, but at the end of the day you have to know your heart and what's best for the whole community in the long run.

We are a five-member commission, and all five are elected at large. We appoint a mayor and a mayor pro tem each April from among us. In the past, the positions have been rotated, and the mayor pro tem has moved into the position of mayor after a term.

I was mayor pro tem in the 2009-'10 term, and I thought that I had performed well. I had a list of initiatives I wanted to pursue once appointed mayor, including a constituent cookout and a reading program at one of the local elementary schools. I had spent the entire year thinking of things that I wanted to do and was excited to take on the new task as mayor, believing that I could do good things for the community in that role.

I was a student at Ottawa University by then. My roommate was excited to be able to tell her friends that her roommate is the mayor. I was launching a bid for student body president as well, and my slogan was going to be, "Let the mayor be your president!"

About two weeks before it was time to appoint a new mayor, I received a call that informed me that a few commissioners had some concerns. So I went and talked to them. They expressed that they didn't think that I would have enough time to be mayor as a college student. I told them it was no different from any of them having a family and a full-time job and that I was going to be taking fewer hours at the university.

That was the only concern that was brought up, and I thought I handled it effectively.

Two days before the official vote for mayor, I started hearing other concerns, which I had not heard before and wish had been presented to me earlier. The eldest commissioner, eighty-one years old, said, "I have heard from other people that they are concerned that you are too immature for the position."

I told him that I didn't think that I had presented myself in a negative light and asked why "other people" said I was immature. He did not have an answer. I told him I thought that as part of the natural progression of my service on the commission, it was my time to become mayor. I was ready and willing to take on the position full force.

The conversation on the commission about who would be mayor was not in my favor. There was an indication that consensus among the commissioners was desired, but I knew I wasn't going to let that happen. I left the session pretty upset.

On the night of the official vote, the woman I had planned to support for mayor pro tem was nominated for mayor and quickly seconded. "All those in favor say aye." Everyone except me did. "All opposed say nay— motion carries" came out in one sweeping statement. I made my nay vote boldly and forcefully, wanting to make clear that I was not okay with how things were being handled.

I sat there in disbelief, especially as I thought about the discussion we had had two nights earlier, in which all seemed to buy into the concept of working toward consensus on important decisions. At least my nay vote let them know that I was not okay with the way I felt treated.

After the issue about my immaturity, it felt ironic that I was then reappointed mayor pro tem. And that I was congratulated for having just been elected president of the student body at Ottawa University.

Advice

Never doubt yourself. I've learned a lot about myself through this process. I've discovered that I can do a lot more than I thought I could, and I can have influence on someone or a group of people that can make an impact. I can take leadership to another level. A lot of young people feel like they can't do it, but obviously we can.

When I made the decision to run for City Commission, I got some criticism, but I never doubted that I could do it. And still now, I believe it's one of the best decisions I have made. I'm twenty years old, and I already know about zoning, roads, and how to manage a $9 million budget. A lot of my classmates can't grasp that concept.

There are hard decisions, and you just have to make them. I think one of the most important things I've learned is that people will talk about you and what you've done, but at the end of the day you have to know you have done the right thing.

I think the impact of our generation is going to be huge. We saw more youth come out for the Obama-McCain election than any other in recent years. More young people are taking notice, and the mindset is changing.

I think those people in Congress who are sixty, seventy, eighty, ninety have a huge disconnect with the younger people today. Older opinions on issues like gay marriage are much different from those of younger people. It varies by party, but lots of laws may change, with lots more diversity and movement toward being progressive and inclusive. I have high hopes for our generation to change things. I'm excited to see where the future takes us and how much we can accomplish.

Serving in public office is a constant balancing act. I'm a U.S. citizen and a state citizen, as well as a tribal citizen. How do I represent all three interests to the highest degree? How do I translate our community's values and conditions into this decision-making process? How do I balance the tribal sovereignty aspect, too? Sometimes you just have to do the best you can, but it doesn't always work out the way you want.

Kevin Killer
South Dakota House of Representatives

History

MY DAD, WHO GREW UP IN Pine Ridge and had to go through lots of hardship living on the reservation, had a major influence on me. He was able to move away and attend the University of South Dakota, getting a degree and becoming a CPA [certified public accountant]. He moved his business to Denver, where I was born and grew up, but he wanted to make sure that I knew my family, so I visited them on the Pine Ridge Reservation every summer.

My grandmother, who I remember as a sincere and loving person, was especially instrumental in my life. I had a great time at her house, which was in the countryside and so open—quite a contrast from our home in Denver. One of the things I found out after she had passed away was she was really involved in the American Indian Movement (AIM), which was kind of like the Black Panthers for native communities.

When I was growing up, I had no idea she was in AIM, and it was really surprising when I found out. I had heard stories about it, but I never really understood the dynamics until I got more politically engaged and began to learn about how it impacted my community. The Wounded Knee massacre happened on the Pine Ridge Reservation in 1890. Wounded Knee II, a confrontation between AIM and the U.S. Government over terrible conditions on the reservation, happened in 1973, and my grandmother was involved in that. She came from a legacy of trying to help people and passed it on to my father, who passed it on to me.

I'm an Oglala Sioux. Our name, Killer, was originally White Buffalo Killer. But when white people or non-native speakers came to our reservations and began to interpret our names, they did not have a word for Buffalo. So ours got changed to White Cow Killer. My family went by that name for a number of years, but my great-grandfather just cut it off, and since then everyone has gone by Killer.

My dad did lots of work with native tribes, nonprofits, and schools, helping them with their financial management. That helped me to understand values connected to business and how to help people. A part of me wanted to grow up and be like my dad and join the family business as a CPA. Unfortunately he passed away in 1999 when I was twenty, and I lost my motivation to stay in business.

I floated around for a few years between Pine Ridge and Denver. Then I was offered a job to help my tribe with financial analysis, and I took the position. What struck me was that I was making money for my tribe, while everyone around me was poor. It was frustrating, because I began to see how politics had a lot to do with the decisions being made about allocated resources going back out into the community.

My dad always told me I needed to come back and help my community, no matter what. That's how he raised me, and it has always stuck with me. I eventually quit financial planning altogether. I was flat broke and unemployed for a year and a half, and that experience showed me firsthand how people have to live in Pine Ridge. This is the background so many people on the reservation have endured, and it inspired me in making my own commitment to do something about it.

Politics

ABOUT THIRTY THOUSAND PEOPLE LIVE ON the Pine Ridge Reservation, and half of our population is under eighteen years old. The unemployment rate is around 80 percent. Many families have no electricity, water, or phones and still use wood-burning stoves to cook meals. Life expectancy in the area is one of the worst in the Western Hemisphere. Over 40 percent of the population has diabetes. Adolescent suicide is four times the national average, and infant mortality is five times the national average. These realities are what motivated me to take on a leadership role.

I started working as a field organizer in Tom Daschle's campaign for U.S. Senate in 2004. The Daschle campaign hired a bunch of young native people, and it was probably the first time many had a job making ten dollars an hour and working forty hours a week. As I went around asking people to register to vote, I began to see the real needs up close.

We had a record turnout in the 2004 election. I was honored that my community was willing to allow me to ask them to vote for certain candidates and to trust me enough to do that. I didn't grow up on the reservation, and my family didn't have to struggle as much as many have. In the beginning, learning their stories wasn't easy, but over time the trust grew.

Having young people come out of those conditions makes it hard to explain why they should vote at all, much less for any senator. In the beginning of the campaign, many of them didn't know a lot about Sen. Daschle. But by the end they had learned who he was, what his values were, and what issues were important to him, including the concerns of Native communities and young people. To see that growth among the young people on the reservation showed me that they really care about their communities and that they want to make them better.

The job with the Daschle campaign was a godsend for me. It made me a more grounded person and a better advocate for the needs of our community. The campaign experience taught me that we needed more people involved; we needed more help. It told me that I really needed to stay here and do more.

I remember a specific conversation I had with another worker on the campaign. I told her I was thinking about going to Washington to work if Sen. Daschle won reelection. She began begging me to stay, saying that the people in our area needed me. When Sen. Daschle didn't win, I stayed in the community, but I did not understand her plea at the time. Now I do. Four years later I understand why talented people are needed here. I think realizing how you can use your magnitude of talents to help is so important.

Campaigning

MY EXPERIENCE WITH THE DASCHLE CAMPAIGN paid off, because some of those workers became part of my campaign staff in 2008. I had decided to run for state representative at a Young People For (YP4) conference, which gathered student activists from across the country. I started talking to some of my mentors, like Joel Silverman, Iara Ping, and Andrew Gillum from the Young Elected Officials network.

The confidence they had and the support they gave me helped me believe I was ready to run. They all gathered around a table with friends and colleagues who had lots of campaign experience, and they started asking me questions. I was able to handle all of them. They said, "Well, we need to find some financial resources." I received support to run a very strong campaign.

I went through a campaign training program called the Front Line Leaders Academy (FLLA), through People for the American Way. Through that experience I was able to meet people from all over the country, and they helped me believe I had a shot to win. They helped with my analysis and designing my literature and other important campaign pieces. I was astonished by how it all came together. Some of the first phone calls I made after I realized I was going to win were to my FLLA friends, to thank them for everything they did to help me.

I had almost dropped out of FLLA because my mom, who has been so important to me, had a stroke in 2006, and I was taking care of her. When I first took her to the hospital, we had to wait two hours before she could be seen by a doctor, because our health-care system is so bad. She then had to be moved to a hospital an hour-and-a-half drive away to be seen. That reminded me of why I was preparing to run for office.

But initially when I came back home from FLLA, I just wanted to help other candidates. I wasn't really sure I wanted to win myself. I had a personal disdain for politics, even though I believed we needed it. And I just didn't know if I would be a good enough candidate. What I came to realize was that anyone could be a candidate, but it's your commitment to your community that is going to show in the long run.

We knew in my campaign that with a dynamic on the reservation of a young population and an 80 percent unemployment rate, there was great tension. Something was going to have to give. Trying to find opportunities for young people is really a challenge, but it became a central part of my campaign.

Even though I had elders to help me out, I think the main energy in my campaign was that young people had something to believe in, and it gave them hope. You see the kids growing up in these conditions, in a community where a lot of the families are living off Social Security. The first of the month, when the checks come in, seems to be a good time. But a large number of the adults drink or otherwise self-medicate, because they are just trying to deal with being unemployed and living in these conditions.

But you can see these young children in our schools. They get up every single day because they believe something is going to change. They believe that their lives are going to get better, and they go through their childhood and teenage years with that hope.

After you hear the stories over and over and over again, the challenge becomes how to translate those stories into positive action, to help them change their lives for the better, so they can empower themselves and fundamentally see that they can do better together. If they can make change happen—see the future and have the power to say this is how we want it rather than being told this is how it is—that is real change. That is something very powerful.

I have a friend who has two children. She helped day and night on my campaign because she really believed in me. Volunteers came to work every single day and helped me. One of my campaign volunteers under thirty told me he looked at me and said to himself, "Hey, maybe he can change something."

During my campaign, I thought it was important to inform voters of their choices. There was a presidential primary at the same time as my election, and that was really good. I was able to work for Barack Obama's campaign on the reservation. It was great that we had all of this exposure through politics and heightened awareness of the issues.

I also enrolled in Oglala Lakota College, one of the first tribally controlled colleges in the United States. It has grown from a community college offering associates' degrees to an institution offering baccalaureate degrees and a master's program in Lakota leadership, bringing hope for innovation and entrepreneurship to build up our economy. I served as the student representative on the College Board of Trustees, which gave me another understanding of leadership.

There were four candidates in the primary election in a two-seat race. I was the top vote getter by a margin of fifteen votes. I won the general election by seven hundred votes. I was twenty-nine.

At first the Legislature was a little intimidating, because you run a campaign on ideals, but those ideals go up against the magnitude of a legislative institution and its process. Serving in public office is a constant balancing act. I'm a U.S. citizen and a state citizen, as well as a tribal citizen. How do I represent all three interests to the highest degree? How do I translate our community's values and conditions into this decision-making process? How do I balance the tribal sovereignty aspect, too? Sometimes you just have to do the best you can, but it doesn't always work out the way you want.

The important thing is not whether your colleagues are Democrats or Republicans but that you see people who actually care. The challenge is to find common ground on the things that we all care about and flush those issues out. Serving on the Judiciary and the Education Committees has shown me how people really make decisions. I've benefited from the learning process so much. It's like one of the best graduate schools in the world, coupled with an interesting soap opera.

I represent the third most impoverished county in the United States. My constituents, who have firsthand knowledge of what it's really like, sent me to the Legislature to produce ideas on how to eradicate poverty. I think the sheer magnitude of how impoverished this area is raises many resource issues. Many businesses have to build from the ground up. That takes a huge capital expenditure, and most small businesses can't afford it, especially in Pine Ridge, where there's no infrastructure at all except government offices. There's just our tribe and the U.S. Government, the Bureau of Indian Affairs and its treaties and laws.

Because the Legislature is such a pro-business environment, it benefited me growing up with my father. I have been able to speak some of that language and understand it. That is crucial, because our community needs economic development and jobs. Unless we do preventative actions through job creation, younger people growing up in these conditions will end up in jail, at a great cost to society.

South Dakota has an interesting dynamic. The rural eastern half is getting older in average age, while the reservations are getting younger.

The future workforce is coming from the reservations. How we work with that is going to impact the entire state in every sector of society.

Our community's problems will not be solved overnight, but we can take steps to slowly eradicate some of these conditions over time. The recession certainly does not help matters any, but at least we can make laws around economic development easier in some communities and look at programs that improve education.

I had a constituent, an older gentleman, come to me one day and say, "Kevin, we need more jobs and to do more things for our community." When I asked if he had any ideas, he responded with specific ones, and I appreciated it. He told me that because of earlier treaties, a particular area was originally part of our homeland. He wanted to pursue a tax on the state to help stimulate the economy, pay us back for what was taken, and create a fund to develop the most impoverished counties. Neither the gentleman nor I knew at the time that a state senator was working on the same concept, under the idea of rural empowerment communities. He even had the legislation laid out.

To be in a position to understand people's ideas and try to figure out what works within the legislative process is such a great gift and opportunity. I now see all the opportunities that I've been given because I have stayed here. I just feel like I need to stay in the community and help until I'm not needed anymore.

Advice

THE BEST POLITICAL ADVICE I'VE EVER gotten is "Your word is your bond." You have to make sure that you not only say what you're going to do, but you do what you say you're going to do. At the end of the day, if you do not do what you say you're going to do in the Legislature, what is the use in you being there?

I think young people should not be afraid to run for office. Nothing in life is guaranteed. There's a chance you could lose, but you might also win. I think the benefits of running for office far outweigh the cost, because you learn so much about the issues in your community. It increases your aptitude on issues, and even your values are challenged. Go into it with an open mind and don't be so stuck on your values that you can't work with anyone.

Don't look at people just as Democrats or Republicans but as people with whom you can find common ground on issues you care about. You can't find common ground all the time as a progressive or a conservative, but it's important to have the reputation that you can work with a variety of people and be effective. I believe I've had some success bringing visibility to the issues in my district.

Being able to look at things in a different way and having constituents look at some of the issues of the Legislature is enlightening, too. Hopefully, we can build a bridge between our community, our tribe, and the Legislature. There will always be roadblocks on all sides, but it is important to get past that and know that we are constantly building our future.

It will take us generations to fully address these issues, and that is the toughest part. We are so shortsighted in our budgeting cycles in the Legislature, because they're only for one year, and many of these problems have been going on for many generations. I make sure I remember that, because it's not all about us; it is for future generations—to ensure that our children have a better foundation.

I want to lead through example with my constituents, working with people from different economic, social, and racial circumstances to break through the biases that generally create polarizing issues. The most important lesson is the one I learned as a kid riding my bike throughout St. Louis: We cannot allow fear to control our hearts. Sometimes we need to lean into our discomfort to do what we can to make change happen.

Shane Cohn
Alderman, St. Louis, Missouri

History

I GREW UP IN THE SUBURBS outside St. Louis. When I was a kid, I had a map that covered my bedroom wall—ten by fourteen feet—of the city of St. Louis. On the wall next to it, I hung a large flag of the city. I subscribed to the *City Journal*, which included minutes from the Board of Aldermen and other local political news. I tracked everything that was happening.

In middle school I carried around a Bible and read it regularly. In high school I carried around copies of the Constitution of the United States and of the state of Missouri. I was so moved by those documents.

I used to ride my bike down to the city, to Forest Park, which is three times bigger than Central Park in New York and was then the largest urban park in North America. It was basically my backyard. The city's art and history museums and other cultural institutions were open to the public for free, and I would hang out in them in the afternoons and on the weekends.

I would also ride into communities downtown. At that point, downtown St. Louis had an abundance of underutilized buildings. Many were vacant and boarded up. I was always fascinated with history and architecture, and I read volumes and volumes about the city of St. Louis: how suburban sprawl happened, "white flight," and the creation of federal and social programs that had an impact on urban neighborhoods. I had all this knowledge at a young age and developed a great passion for St. Louis.

When I got home from those trips into the city, my mom would freak out and try to ground me. But I use them now as examples to show that I never let fear control my heart. Sometimes we need to lean into our discomfort to do what we can to make change happen.

When I was nineteen, I enlisted in the military. While I was waiting to start my service, I began to accept my sexual orientation. So just as I was coming to terms with it and coming out of the closet, I was thrown into a system where I was told day after day that I needed to conform, to "be a soldier."

I went through basic training, but I was trying to identify with my own individuality, and the Army isn't exactly about that. Being told to conform to policies that were not welcoming to me tremendously impacted not only my ability to serve, which was compromised by the systematic oppression, but also impacted me psychologically and emotionally as well.

After basic training, I realized I would never be able to be honest about who I was in the Army. One of the core values in the Army is duty. I remember drafting an essay on what Army values meant to me. Don't you have a duty to yourself on a basic human level, just as much as you do to others? If you can't serve in an environment where you are accepted, how are you going to be able to serve others or your country?

I ended up leaving the military after eight months of service and took a job working in the field of human resources. I cannot tell you how grateful I am that Don't Ask Don't Tell has been overturned. My decision to leave the Army was directly connected to the culture created by that obscene policy.

Politics

I BEGAN BY BEING INVOLVED IN my neighborhood. I was active in my community, helping to revitalize our neighborhood business association and serving on the board of the local, nonprofit Housing Development Corporation. I interfaced with a lot of folks around the city and became very active outside of my neighborhood with other community and advocacy organizations.

The alderwoman who served my ward was very nice—and seventy-four years old—and I began thinking we should develop a succession plan, in the event that she were to retire, or something else were to happen. I initiated some conversations and started reaching out to neighborhood leaders, asking them if they were interested in running. They did not have an interest, but some folks asked me why I wasn't considering it.

At that point I was very involved with work and didn't have the ability to get involved in a campaign. Months later, I was approached again, and I eventually announced my candidacy and then left my job to campaign full-time.

Campaigning

WHEN I LAUNCHED MY CAMPAIGN, I differentiated myself with a message that resonated with my community, because I'd already been actively involved and was a leader in community organizations, helping them with strategic vision. My priorities on the campaign focused on neighborhood safety, youth engagement, and development.

In terms of neighborhood safety, my opponents were talking about crime, which is very reactive. You can put only so many police officers on the streets, and we are limited by financial resources. The very nature of law enforcement is addressing criminal activity once it is witnessed or suspected. It is incumbent upon people to create an active safety environment, being thoughtful about how we do that. I don't think anyone in their heart of hearts believes that governments can solve all their issues, so my messaging around the relationship between neighborhood and youth engagement resonated well with people.

We have an influx of young families in our neighborhoods, and we have a lot of young adults who live in the neighborhoods, and we don't have any resources for them. I was the only person in the campaign that was talking about the young people in the ward. And I was able to connect with older adults who work with younger kids, too. I talked with them about things we can do to help young people in our community have something productive to do with their time.

In terms of development, I served on the Housing Development Corporation's board and have several friends that are developers. Even in this economic environment, development is possible; it just needs to be planned well. It's all about having a strategic plan, creating a vision and leveraging resources to achieve our goals. Messaging and experience were definitely what differentiated me from my opponents.

Union workers supported me, because their ideals are important to me, and the AFL-CIO was very generous to my campaign. And I received the endorsement of *El Mundo Latino*, the bilingual newspaper, and support from the Latino community. *The St. Louis American*, the region's largest African American newspaper, was also supportive of my campaign.

From a campaign tactic perspective, we were completely grassroots. I spent every day going out knocking on doors, chatting with people to understand what their concerns were. I refocused my campaign based on their feedback. And that differentiated me as well.

I ran as an open candidate, but I did not use that as a reason why I should be elected. Heterosexual candidates do not go around screaming "I'm a heterosexual candidate." Why should I go around screaming "I'm a homosexual candidate"? During the campaign, I addressed it on an individual level, but I didn't broadcast it in my mass communications.

I didn't feel the need to directly disclose it on my promotional material or website, but I wasn't hiding anything. If you look at my activities, you'll see that I've been a member of the Human Rights Campaign and served on the board of Pride St. Louis. I just want to be known for who I am, what I've done, and what I envision. I always try to give people the courtesy to be who they are.

I'm not going to lie about who I am to anyone. There were many times on the campaign trail when I was sitting in someone's living room, with a Bible on the coffee table and crosses on the wall, and they would ask me about my orientation, and I would tell them. The one thing I can tell you is that I will always be upfront and honest with you. Even if you don't agree with me being gay, at least maybe we can agree on my vision, and I hope that we can agree to disagree and move forward as neighbors. For the most part, people were really okay with that.

I was canvassing late one evening, trying to reach as many households in my ward as I could. A black female in her fifties answered a door. She had the wooden crosses on the walls and the Bible on the coffee table. She had just received one of my mailings listing my priorities in the campaign.

She started asking me personal questions. She wanted to know if I was married, and I told her I was not. She said, "I have a problem with one of your opponents." I told her that I made a point in my campaign not to speak about my opponents, and certainly not to speak ill of them. She said, "You don't have to, you just have to listen to me."

One of my opponents was sending out mail that mentioned living with a person outside of marriage and their child. The woman I was visiting said that she thought this was inappropriate and that they were living in sin. I was sitting there thinking that if she feels this way about them, how is she going to feel about me when I tell her I'm gay?

I told her that I could appreciate her feelings but that I thought there were many different definitions of family. And I added, "To be honest, I have to let you know that I'm gay."

She just looked at me and said. "Oh honey, I already knew that."

This opponent self-presented as a church-and-family person, who had been called by God to run for public office, and she felt that such statements were contrary to actions, and she appreciated that she didn't see that in me. "I may not think what you're doing is right," she said, "but at least you're honest enough to tell me and not try to make me feel like I'm an idiot."

The opponent was executing smear tactics against me, trying to play into fear and stereotypes by referring to me as a "gay activist" and going into the businesses that displayed signs supporting my candidacy, many of them minority-owned, thinking it could set them off. But these were people who knew me through my work on boards and in the neighborhood, with whom I had built strong rapport. And their response in every case was essentially, "We don't care, Shane is our guy."

As a gay male, I can identify with people in terms of oppression. I had many conversations with women and people of different ethnicities and races. People told me that they found me compassionate and able to identify with them on a personal level, and I believe that negated the bias that may have been there otherwise.

Like many communities across the country, we launched a local NOH8

(No Hate) campaign in response to the passage of Proposition Eight in California in November 2008 [which defined marriage as only between a man and a woman]. As a result of Prop Eight and similar efforts, those wonderful, beautiful state constitutional documents, written to protect the rights and privileges of all society, now have discrimination enshrined into their language. It is a horribly disgusting thing when viewed through the values of freedom and equality.

Our local initiative was called NOH8 Project St. Louis. The effort gained lots of momentum after an act of violence against several young gay guys who were leaving a club in St. Louis. They were assaulted by heterosexual guys leaving another nightclub across the street. The St. Louis Project organized fundraisers to help pay the medical expenses of the victims.

There was also a march, with more than 150 people participating, which started in an up-and-coming, gay-friendly neighborhood and ended at City Hall. I was honored to speak to the crowd, acknowledging that the moment was another rallying cry along the journey for progress in our community.

I recently submitted an amendment to a bill that requires any businesses and contractors on public works projects over $1 million to have a personnel policy in place that is nondiscriminatory and inclusive of gay, lesbian, bisexual, and transgender persons, which is huge. Many of these companies are family-owned construction firms. The bill passed unanimously from committee and passed the Board of Aldermen.

Being on the Board of Aldermen has been wonderful and a learning experience. I am having a great opportunity to influence change in the city of St. Louis and hopefully other parts of Missouri as well. In the last session, I sponsored a bill called the Complete Streets Law, which essentially instituted a policy that helps create healthy communities through the city's design review process on infrastructure improvement. Concepts such as "walk-ability" and "bike-ability," along with multimodal transit outside of the automobile will now be systematically brought into all design processes for review.

Our very active biking community in St. Louis gave me good reviews. I have an automobile, but my primary form of transportation is my legs, and I also enjoy my bike. I also take public transportation. When you're talking about development in the city, there are two things that every good system of commerce wants to see: good transportation and an educated populace. Transportation and public education are two very important concerns of mine.

We are working with neighborhood-based organizations to hire a real-estate and business-development officer, who will catalog commercial properties throughout the area, collecting information for potential developers and businesses that may want to occupy those buildings. We started a loan program for new businesses that locate in our neighborhoods. We have some infrastructure enhancements in commercial districts started through the national Recovery Act, including installing energy-efficient streetlights.

I began with a very neighborhood-based campaign focused on neighborhood-based solutions. But during the debates and forums, I began to see that as an alderman I would need to be also focused on city-wide issues. My campaign rekindled the fondness I've always had for the city of St. Louis. As an alderman, I'm amazed at how massive city government is, and the job isn't always easy.

I got bombarded with phone calls after a local news affiliate aired a segment about fire hydrants being painted in a neighborhood in my ward that wanted to do some simple beautification efforts. The reporter twisted the story by saying that the fire department was facing layoffs, "and there's this alderman going around painting fire hydrants." What he failed to mention was that the monies for the painting of the fire hydrants came from sales tax revenue that was publicly approved by the taxpayers of St. Louis for infrastructure enhancements only. And that while other city departments took an across-the-board, ten percent cut, the fire department was one of two departments that had an increase in their budget approved by the Board of Aldermen.

The people who live in my ward and saw the TV segment called to say, "Nice job, alderman! We love you! Glad to see you are doing a great job helping the neighborhood. We love the hydrants." But I also got phone calls from people all over the region saying, "How dare you paint fire hydrants?" A great number of them were from wives of firefighters.

I could understand their concern. It was unfortunate that I gave the reporter two interviews and all that showed up was this two-minute segment that omitted most of the relevant information. After I explained the background to people, their response would be, Oh, I guess I can understand why you would support that, and I wasn't even expecting you to actually call me back. A lot of people just don't expect their elected officials to return their calls.

One woman asked why we couldn't just have volunteers do the project. I told her, "Ma'am, there are more than four hundred hydrants." And on the week she called, the temperature was 100 degrees on average.

I told her that there were still a number of hydrants that needed to be painted, and that if she wanted to volunteer to hunch over and paint them in the 100 degree weather, she was more than welcome to do so.

She then said, "Oh, I didn't mean me! I meant the people in the neighborhood." I told her that I thought the people in the neighborhood probably felt the same way she did. At that point she just let it go.

I went to an older colleague whose career as alderwoman spanned basically my entire life. I asked her to tell me the trick I need to know to survive this kind of stuff. She said there really is not a trick, and no matter what you do there will always be some backlash. She said, "Shane, I've been here for twenty-five years, and I'm still learning stuff every day. You are never going to know everything."

Whether fire hydrants or Don't Ask Don't Tell, it all comes down to human nature and change. I have twelve thousand constituents, and I get tons of phone calls, positive and negative, about issues ranging from dog poop to development. Either way, people are going to call.

Advice

BE YOURSELF. TOO OFTEN I SEE people who want to get involved in politics with motives that are self-serving, often because they just want to have a career in politics. Be yourself and be a servant leader, and don't view your position as merely a stepping stone to higher office. Understanding who you are and the needs of your community and working for the betterment of that community are important.

One helpful piece of advice that was offered to me was, "Find your voice before it is given to you"—either on the campaign trail or in governing. That goes along with understanding who you are and refining your message, letting people know who you are before you are influenced by others. Once you're elected, they come at you from all different directions, wanting to sway you in theirs. You have to know your values, know who you are and what's important for your neighborhoods and constituents, and have that voice so that you can stand firm and vote with a good conscience.

Understanding your limits is important. Being a public servant can consume as much time as you give it. I'm a very dedicated, hard-working person, and so I can easily go twenty hours a day. I'm learning that I'm not omnipresent. It is definitely a challenge, and there are a lot of expectations placed on elected officials to be everywhere all the time. Creating time for myself is something that is very important. It's necessary to keep from getting burned out.

Because of the accessibility of technology in our culture today, young people are exposed to a lot more than previous generations. That knowledge and experience has had a very defining impact on my generation. Utilizing technology to communicate and build relationships and be more open with constituents is something that is very different in terms of moving equality forward for our generation and can be a great tool. But too often technology removes the relationships and focuses on communication, which is different from building relationships. It shouldn't take away from that face-to-face time and the dialogue that is necessary.

I want to lead through example with my constituents in working with people from different economic, social, and racial circumstances to break through the biases that generally create polarizing issues. The most important lesson is the one I learned as a kid riding my bike into St. Louis: We cannot allow fear to control our hearts.

I got interested in politics when I began attending a community college, the summer before I started high school. My favorite class was American government. I was barely fourteen years old, and I was so short that I had to stand on a milk crate to see over the podium, when I gave my class presentation on a Supreme Court case about criminalizing sodomy between two men in Texas. I got an A. The professor wrote on my paper that I handled a very difficult subject with a lot of calm and without any embarrassment. Yeah, because I had no idea what sodomy was!

Kyrsten Sinema
Arizona State Senate

History

I WAS BORN IN TUCSON, ARIZONA, and grew up in a family of very conservative Mormon Republicans. My father taught me to read when I was two years old. When I was five, I told him that I was tired of my "dumb and silly" little kids' books. I wanted a real book.

His library was the one room in the house where we kids weren't allowed to go. But he took me into that room, which had books literally from the floor to the ceiling, and he told me I could pick whatever I wanted. I chose *Roots*, by Alex Haley.

I read that book in kindergarten. I believe that it fundamentally shaped how I see the world. I certainly was not old enough to understand the significance of the entire story, but I did understand the deep level of injustice that was a key thread throughout the book. I got an early exposure to themes of redemption and overcoming obstacles.

Incidentally, I also read Stephen King's *It* when I was a child, and I'm still afraid of clowns, shower curtains, and drains! Being encouraged to read allowed me to have a very inquisitive mind and the freedom to learn whatever I wanted. I grew up absorbing information, and that taught me to think critically. I was an insatiable reader, beginning with the cereal box in the morning. Whenever my mother felt she needed to punish me, she made me put down the book I was reading and go outside.

My mom, who was raised by a Mexican American woman who lived next door to her family, grew up eating Mexican food and speaking Spanish. I was about seven when I figured out that I was Anglo and not Latino, and I was just devastated. Someone called me a *gringa*, and I was really upset. That was when I realized that race was a factor in our community.

My parents had divorced when I was five, and I split my time between them. When I was eight, my mother and stepfather moved to a small town in northwest Florida. There the racism was in-your-face blatant. The train tracks literally divided the whites on one side from the blacks on the other. I went to school in Florida and spent summers and vacations in Tucson. It was like culture shock every time I got on the plane.

When I was in seventh grade, my parents were going out of town one weekend, and they asked me to pick someone to stay with. I chose a good friend, one of the very few African Americans in the Mormon Church. At the end of the school day, I got on the bus with her, and we headed toward the other side of the tracks. People began throwing rocks at the window, because it was unheard-of for a white kid to be getting on that bus.

That was very, very difficult for me. I remember thinking that there was something terribly wrong. Racism wasn't something we talked about, so I had to figure out how to deal with it. Such experiences in my childhood helped form what I think is the driving force of who I am today and what gets me out of the bed in the morning: social justice.

They also taught me how to be strong and on my own in the face of opposition. I had a different political outlook from many of my friends. I was very much alone growing up, but the good news was that the small-town environment helped me to be comfortable with it and to be confident in who I am and not worry about what others thought. It helped me build a very strong sense of self.

But I also learned that a small town didn't have a lot to offer me intellectually and socially. When I was in middle school, I started thinking about how to get out of there. Seriously, it was in sixth grade. It was around the time that a teacher told me that I had to take a home economics class.

I was like, "No, no. That's not going to work for me."

The response was, "This is what all the girls do."

And I was like, "Not this girl!"

By junior high, I was actively plotting how to get out. I actually began attending community college before I started high school. My older brother had to take some summer classes at Okaloosa Walton Community College in order to graduate from high school. I told him and my parents that I wanted to go, too.

Politics

I ENROLLED IN CLASSES AND MADE the forty-five-minute drive with my brother to the community college every day. The summer before I entered high school, I took American government, calculus, and chemistry. The best part was American government.

Each student had the opportunity to pick two Supreme Court cases to research. But I missed the first day of classes because my stepfather got food poisoning on a trip to Texas, and we were late getting back to Florida. When I returned, I was assigned the only two cases left. One was about the death penalty.

The other was *Bowers vs. Hardwick*. I was barely fourteen years old, and I was so short that I had to stand on a milk crate to see over the podium when I gave my class presentation about criminalizing sodomy between two men in Texas. I got an A. At the end of the class, the professor wrote on my paper that I handled a very difficult subject with a lot of calm and without any embarrassment. Yeah, because I had no idea what sodomy was!

By the time I was a junior in high school, I had all the credits I needed to graduate from high school with an associate's degree. So I went off to college when I was sixteen. I finished with a bachelor's degree in social work when I was eighteen.

Then I went to live in Kenya for a few months. I did mostly organizational development work in a community outside of Mombasa on the southeast coast. I focused on education and literacy and also did some work in basic hygiene and preventable diseases.

I returned to Arizona, where I worked with Mexican immigrants in a barrio in north-central Phoenix. My job was helping refugee kids navigate an often unwelcoming school environment. I was eighteen when I started. I wore wire-rim glasses to try to look older. At nineteen I was teaching parenting classes.

My first year in social work was very difficult and depressing. Families were coming with these incredible needs: lack of English language, lack of housing, and lack of rights because they were not citizens and didn't have legal access to the system. During that time, I was glad that as a child I had experienced poverty in a way that helped me to understand it.

After my parents divorced, I lived for two years with my mother in an abandoned gas station without running water or electricity. I remember going to school and being deeply ashamed because I had nothing. I wanted to be cool and have all the nice things. The other kids had Keds and nice clothes, and I wore hand-me-downs from a girl that was two years older than me. At church she would say to me, "That's my old dress." It was so embarrassing. But that experience helped me understand and put a frame around what is important in life and what is not.

After a year as a social worker, I got really depressed because I thought I was only putting band-aids on a much larger problem. I could see all of the societal injustices, such as institutionalized discrimination, and I didn't have the tools to do anything about it. So I went back to school at night to get my master's degree.

That helped, because it taught me to look at the larger perspective: the idea that you work with communities to create societal change and social justice, rather than just solve people's individual problems. I eventually became the lead social worker in my school district, running a family resource center and writing multimillion-dollar grants. But one day I just realized that I had done all that I could do in that job.

By this time I was doing a lot of political work in the community—not electoral work, but activist work. I was working on civil rights, equal rights, and environmental justice. And I kept seeing the roots of the problems percolating up in the communities I served.

So I went to get coffee one day with a brilliant friend of mine at the Sierra Club. She suggested that I go to law school. I thought she was absolutely right, that that's what I had to do. Law school taught me to process and analyze information in a way that has been one of the most valuable skills I've learned in my life. And it gave me access to power that has historically been denied the communities I have served.

It was a busy two and a half years—not three, because I like to move fast. I graduated three weeks after I was elected to the Arizona State House of Representatives at the age of twenty-seven. Now I'm in the middle of my PhD.

Campaigning

MY CAMPAIGN STRATEGY WAS A COMMUNITY organizing strategy: make contact, and make friends with everyone you talk to. Listen to them and let them know that you're going to deliver. That's what made the difference for me.

On primary night of my first election, I had a party at my house, and I was very nervous. But my volunteers just kept coming in my door, wearing their Sinema T-shirts and telling me how great it had been to be part of my campaign. They had spent the day handing out cards at the polling places. Many of them told me that every person they handed a card to said something like, "Oh, I know Kyrsten; she came to my door." I have chills again just thinking about it.

I had hundreds of volunteers who were not political operatives. Most were people who had never been into politics before. Some had never voted. A lot of them didn't even like politics. I thought, *Wow, these people are here because they believe in me, and because they believe that we can do something bigger and better than has been done before.* We were making people feel that they have a stake in this process. I thought, *God, I'm so glad I did this.* It was a wonderful moment.

That night I came in first place in the primary. So, I got elected. And then I showed up for work to do all these great things for my community, and the Republicans were like, "Honey, you can go sit in a corner." They patted me on my head and sent me on my way. My first year was horrible.

In order to change, I had to send myself through a ring of fire. I was soul-searching, asking myself: What do I want to do? Is this a good use of my time? I felt totally ineffective, like my hands were tied, and I wasn't helping the people I was supposed to help.

Then I realized that I was just approaching it the wrong way. Once I learned how to approach it differently, I was totally changed. Now I feel very successful in my job, and I get a lot done. I achieve the majority of the goals I set out to achieve.

An example of how things changed was around gay marriage. Five days after I was elected, members of the leading gay group in the state called a meeting and invited me to it. They were looking for someone to lead the effort to defeat the bill banning gay marriage. Everyone else in the room pulled their chairs back, so there I was.

I had to learn over time how to build a coalition. We built a massive one, with police officers and firefighters, churches and seniors, libertarians. We learned how to frame our message in such a way that it didn't seem stereotypical. I took a lot of heat from a lot of gay groups and individuals who were upset because we were using a mainstream framing and a mainstream message. I'm bisexual, and it was hard to feel that pushback from my own community. But I don't regret my strategy for a second.

Arizona is in the spotlight right now, because of our recent legislation targeting immigrants. It is very difficult to live in a state that endorses racial profiling. It is hard to live where attitudes and behaviors that I believe are immoral are so widely accepted.

When I was a teenager, I was obsessed with the civil rights movement. I was living in the Deep South, and I read everything about it. I remember agonizing and wondering, if I'd been alive during that time, what would I have done? Would I have gone to Selma? To Birmingham? Would I have put my life on the line?

I wanted to think that I am the kind of person who would have done that. But when I imagined myself in that time, I wondered, what if I was not courageous? What if I was too afraid?

I don't wonder that anymore. Because Arizona is Selma right now. I know now that I would have done just what I'm doing right here, right now: bearing witness to what is occurring, and doing what I can with the small amount of power that I have to speak out and to call attention and to name it for what it is. I want to make sure that when history records what is happening now in Arizona, it will do so with the knowledge that many of us stood up and said, This is wrong; this is immoral.

I didn't think that I would ever have the opportunity to make a decision like this in my life. I mean, the civil rights movement was so big, and I had no idea that there would be anything of that magnitude in my lifetime. But I believe that the right of immigrants to live and work and be in this country is ultimately that struggle. I know that I'm doing what needs to be done. Every day I feel like I'm doing my best with the power that I have to change what is going on.

Advice

IT TAKES TIME TO LEARN HOW to navigate the political system and do it effectively. There is nothing worse than seeing someone who has great talent but has not developed the skill to maneuver the system well. And so they marginalize themselves or allow themselves to be marginalized. That's what I did to myself my first year.

I revamped the way that I work, and now my values and morals are still rock solid, but I've learned how to win. Which is so much better than losing. You can become politically very successful without sacrificing a single ounce of your morality or your values. You can. Never give up anything you believe in, but be smart and develop the skill sets you need to be effective in getting what you need for your community.

Unity became our strategy for developing the political power necessary to truly take transformative action where people had given up on the idea of transformation even being possible. We stressed that unity does not mean that we give up all of our differences; it just means that we commit to a larger purpose—which in our case was student achievement. We created this tent that was big enough for everyone. And when we had an event, we would bring them all together, and people would be in the same room and say, "Wait a minute, I'm on the same side as *who?*"

Airick Leonard West, President
Kansas City School Board

History

IF THERE IS ONE THING THAT I'm absolutely, unshakably clear about, it's that I was given a remarkable blessing at birth. I was placed in a foster family with Dick and Linda Crabill, two of the most amazing people I've ever had the privilege of knowing. I know so many horror stories of the foster care system, and unfortunately I am the owner of a few of those, but under their care I knew nothing but love. Any amount of character, any measure of integrity, any goodness that is a component of who I am as a person today has its genesis on their farm near Joplin, in the very conservative southwest corner of Missouri.

I did a lot of bouncing around in my childhood, but in my first five years I knew family, the only consistent example of family I have ever known. The Crabills were raising a household of thirteen children, with only three of them being their own. I absolutely loved my childhood on the farm. We worked hard, raising cattle, baling hay, and growing most of our food. We always had canned or frozen something, and what we didn't have, we traded for with our neighbors.

A sense of community and mutuality and the interconnectedness of us all was hard to miss in a household of fifteen, but it extended beyond our home as well. If a neighbor needed assistance getting in crops, we all piled in the truck and headed on down the road to help. When a family's house burned down, we took them in. The Crabills' sense of service and community and an unerringly conservative worldview have been foundational in creating this strange guy who lives in the heart of Kansas City's inner city and talks about personal responsibility and community as avenues to improving education.

My early teenage years in rural Missouri had its challenges. When I was in middle school, I was the only African American in the school I attended. I was beaten up by another kid whose family had sympathies with the KKK [Ku Klux Klan] and heckled regularly on the football field.

I decided to go my own way and moved back to Kansas City when I was sixteen years old. By the time I graduated high school, I had attended eleven different schools. I periodically worked odd jobs and lived with friends while I finished school. I lived out of my car at times, until a friend borrowed and wrecked it.

There were days I found myself hanging out at friends' houses until I wore out my welcome. When I'd leave, I would tell them I was going home. I was really going to a vacant house near my school, where I would break in and then put things back without arousing suspicion. Every day I would get up around 6 a.m. and walk to school, showering and washing my clothes in the locker room of the gym every morning. Then I'd go on about my business as though none of that were happening.

I worked in Kansas City as a computer programmer and website designer for a while. I became active in the Ivanhoe neighborhood where I live. As vice-president of my neighborhood association, I got involved in a land-use and redevelopment plan for the area and an effort to get block captains on each of Ivanhoe's four hundred city blocks to address issues of litter and crime. What we found was that when people come together in community, believing in themselves and taking care of each other, all the conditions get better. That wasn't exactly news to me; that was the story of my life.

One thing that had made all the difference for me was that frequently adults who had no reason to be involved in my life chose to be, through mentoring and big-brother programs. Absent the kindness and encouragement of those random strangers, it's clear to me that I would never have graduated from high school and discovered my own leadership potential, much less done anything useful with my life. Those relationships were blessings that God put my way.

My life experiences led me to become a big brother of sorts to a lot of young men in my community. I refer to them as my "gentlemen." They are kids who hang out at my house, elbow onto the computer, and follow me to events. Wherever I go, they go. If I go to neighborhood meetings, they go; if I go to the symphony, they go; if I go horseback riding, they go.

Politics

TWO YEARS AGO, ONE OF THESE young men found himself without support or a place to live. I was single and twenty-eight at the time—and naïve enough to think that I could get the job done and take on a fourteen-year-old kid. That's how I became the guardian of Damon.

He started coming home from school, telling me these horrific stories that I thought could only be the fiction of a teenage mind. They seemed too ridiculous to be believed. I just assumed these were excuses for him not doing what he needed to do in school. But he was persistent with them, so finally I decided to visit his school.

As I sat in the back of his classroom, I was utterly appalled at what I saw. It was a nightmarish scenario, worse than he had described. There were as many security officers as teachers, and still there were fights, and absolutely no education was going on.

I started volunteering at the school. I joined the Parents' Association, and then became the head of it. In that role, I tried to reach out and engage the parents of other scholars at the school. I eventually found myself speaking before the School Board, side by side with the principal, about the severity of the situation. I remember begging the School Board to do something about it. I don't think I ever felt more unheard in my life.

I started to look for people to run for the School Board. I had this great slate of guys to run. They were all jazzed about it, and we were good to go. But there was one small problem; they were all married, and their forays into public office were put on hold by their wives. They basically said to me: Well, we can't do it, but you're single, so why don't you do it?

Campaigning

OF THE NINE SEATS ON THE Kansas City School Board, six are district seats and three are at large. Four were up for election that year. Running unopposed for my district seat would have made more political sense and been much easier. But my intention was always more about sparking a conversation than promoting myself or winning a campaign. In fact, the name of the campaign committee that we filed with the state was Kansas Citians United for Educational Achievement—not the Committee to Elect Airick Leonard West or something like the normative stuff.

I wanted to initiate a widespread community conversation around the question: What would happen in Kansas City if we were united for the educational achievement of our scholars? In order to engage that topic on a citywide scale, I needed to run at large. Despite the obstacles, I stuck with my decision.

My opponent was an incumbent who had been appointed to his at-large seat, because no one had filed to run in the previous election, which was sadly typical. This time he actually had to mount a campaign. He had strong support from the business community and was in line to become the chairman of the board. I had people call and tell me he was unbeatable and I shouldn't run against him. I basically told them: You know, I'm probably not going to win, but the story of our schools needs to get out there, and we need to do something about it.

After I filed, people in the know told me that I could have chosen the open seat in my district and been unopposed, pointing out that I was running for the only contested seat in six years. I was such a political neophyte. But my opponent's candidacy was not remotely germane to my message. I wasn't running against anyone; I was running for a specific vision that I was trying to create.

My theme of unity spoke to a starkly divided city of haves and have-nots. The challenge was to mount a different sort of campaign that would bring everybody to the table.

We started moving beyond antiquated notions of separation and stratification by race and class and built a coalition that looked like the entire city. It included a diversity of teenagers and seniors, gay and straight, affluent and poor, Protestants and Catholics and Muslims, black and white and brown. The core of my campaign team embodied that diversity.

Unity became our strategy for developing the political power neces-sary to truly take transformative action, where people had given up on the idea of transformation even being possible. We stressed that unity does not mean that we give up all of our differences; it just means that we commit to a larger purpose—which in our case was student achieve-ment. We created this tent that was big enough for everyone. And when we had an event, we would bring them all together, and people would be in the same room and say: Wait a minute, I'm on the same side as *who?*

My opponent, who was the recently retired dean of the business school at the University of Missouri at Kansas City (UMKC), spent more money on his political consultant than I raised in the entire campaign. But I had been actively involved in the community for years, and I had an amazing campaign manager—who, incidentally, was a department head at UMKC and ran a flawless campaign.

We had hundreds of volunteers out in the community knocking on doors. We were everywhere, handing out flyers at every neighborhood meeting. We knew the conversation needed to spread virally, so we went to neighborhood associations and churches, and we threw lots of house parties to get people together to talk about the quality of education in Kansas City.

I was taken aback by our strength. Having never done this before, I didn't know that the things you need to do to organize a citywide conversation are the same things you need to do if you want to run a very powerful grassroots ground game for an election. After this intense three-month conversation, lo and behold, we walked away with the win. I received just shy of nine thousand votes, which, as best as I can tell, was the largest number of votes for a School Board candidate in thirty years.

Then I had to figure out what to do. How to make a difference.

What I knew about education would not fill the bottom of a thimble. I came to my position knowing that I was the newly drafted guardian for a fourteen-year-old. That was it. I just needed to take care of this kid I loved. The Kansas City school system was beleaguered and in disarray. Our district lost its accreditation about a decade ago, and it was operating under provisional accreditation, with the possibility of the state taking it over if we didn't show significant change.

Many people who lived in the urban core of the city no longer live here, and school enrollment has declined from about eighty thousand students three decades ago to less than twenty thousand today. One of the more remarkable things is that of the nine members of the School Board, only two of us have been elected to our current terms. What has become normative is a degree of apathy so severe that citizens have literally stopped running for office. In one district with more than forty thousand residents, a write-in candidate won with about three hundred votes. The election before mine, in which five School Board seats were to be in play, was canceled because no one ran; all the incumbents were reappointed. It was quite clear that increasing the level of civic engagement needed to be a top priority.

I'm incredibly stubborn. If there weren't this pervasive sense that the restoration of this district is entirely impossible, I don't know if this work would appeal to me as much as it does.

As a child I had learned in practical and intuitive ways the value of family and community. As a teenager, I was alone at times and presented with the very basic need to survive against seemingly overwhelming odds. As a result of that experience, I learned self-reliance and discovered an eternal amount of determination and drive that some, today, may even call ruthlessness in support of our scholars and toward transforming the Kansas City School District. That is because I know the stakes are too high, and these young lives are too important for them to become another statistic in a failed school system.

I had two primary concerns I wanted to pursue on the board. The first concern was how to continue building the conversation about bringing the community together around our public school system. We have done that in a few ways, most notably through an effort we call the BE 1! CAMPAIGN. We have asked people to live up to our responsibility to be personally engaged and invested in the lives of our scholars in a powerful and meaningful way as mentors and tutors.

When we look at what scholars need to be successful, we realize that they are not successes or failures in isolation. Every kid is going to make mistakes. Research shows that the main difference between those scholars that made it and the ones that did not was that there were people that helped pick us back up when we fell down. Those individuals made the caring web of relationships so tight that we did not fall through.

We say that for each of the twenty thousand scholars in the school district to be successful consistent with their potential, they need to be supported by at least five caring individuals. We have partnered with more than fifteen community agencies working with youth, including Big Brothers Big Sisters, Boys & Girls Clubs, and the YMCA. These are familiar organizations that have been involved with the lives of our scholars for years, but we have brought them together in one cohesive conversation. And we've invited anyone who lives, works, worships, or plays within the boundaries of the Kansas City School District to be part of that conversation and to consider being one of those five caring individuals in the life of a child.

My second concern was more challenging. As part of my public service, I've served on a couple dozen nonprofit and city and county boards, and I know what good governance looks like. What hit me on my first day on the job, in my very first committee meeting, was that we did not practice good governance on the School Board. We practiced micromanagement but not really governance.

We spent our time second-guessing the members of the school administration and in most cases telling them how to do their jobs. It was a surprise for me to find out that we had gone through twenty-six school superintendents in forty years. But if you are good at what you do, would you stick around for a board overstepping its bounds and managing you?

I immediately had the impression that our revolving door of superintendents was contributing to our failure to provide achievement for our scholars. And that the micromanaging practices of the board were contributing to the revolving door—actually, in fact, spinning the door faster. The challenge was how to institute good governance practices.

When you have a body that is accustomed to awesome power and personally managing a $400 million budget, how do you convince folks that it's in the best interest of scholars for them to give up that power? I spent my first eighteen months in office trying to build a consensus that we as a board united will walk away from our micromanaging practices and restrain ourselves to governance practices.

What I've been saying is one 100 percent counter to the way the board has done business and to the way the school administration has grown accustomed to being run. We have paid people six-figure salaries to show up in meetings so that a bunch of volunteers can tell them how to do their jobs. I think the board got addicted to power and the administration to enabling it, because it was easy and provided job security and didn't require accountability.

On the School Board we have four-year terms, with no term limits, and people just stay. One person has been on the board over half my lifetime. When I got on the board, I think the other members thought I was a little moody; and they definitely thought I was a little slow.

But slowly, over time, some colleagues came around. After about a year on the job, I thought we probably had the votes to pass the policy reforms necessary to take away the management powers of the board. But it wasn't good enough for me to have a 5-4 or 6-3 vote, because that defies the practice of unity that I ran to embody. I knew that in order to be a catalyst for transformation in the district, we were going to have to find a way for these policy overhauls to be unanimous—despite the fact that we were taking power away from ourselves.

It took a year and a half to get the job done, but the good news is that the comprehensive package of policy reforms I had been advocating passed unanimously. The people in the community just could not believe the changes we were instituting, but we got the job done in no small part because we had a massive grassroots network that had been developed throughout the campaign and remained active. That enabled us to get around what is the most contentious issue a board could possibly face: the revocation of its own powers.

We still retain accountability for casting the vision and offering oversight. The way I have been explaining it to my colleagues conceptually is that we decide where the ship is going, and at the end we decide whether or not we got to where we intended to go. All the rest is up to the superintendent.

A movement is emerging that has required courageous and bold leadership from our community. The be 1! initiative has increased volunteerism in the school district. Kansas Citians United for Educational Achievement hosted a widely successful candidate school, with the intent of being proactive in developing and training a new hoard of emerging leaders and would-be School Board members for the Kansas City School District.

We had a watershed election in 2010, just weeks after the School Board voted to close almost half of our schools due to declining enrollment, poor academic quality, and high administrative and maintenance expenses. A diverse slate of three candidates, endorsed by Kansas Citians United for Educational Achievement and committed to transformation, won more than 70 percent of the district-wide vote. As a result, there is an air of new possibility and momentum that is undeniable. It is crucial that we seize this moment and act quickly.

As the newly elected president of the School Board, I see my central mission at this moment as two-fold. First, it is crucial to continue to embody a vision of widespread community engagement, which is needed to lead our board through the treacherous path ahead and ultimately to reshape our school system to unleash the energy, intellect, and passion of our scholars. Second, we must provide specific leadership to our superintendent through the establishment of clear goals and expectations, along with the support and accountability necessary to transform the Kansas City School District and stand united behind our schools for all of our children.

Advice

IF I'VE LEARNED ANYTHING IN POLITICS, it is that politics is local. If there are any solutions to be found, they are going to be found locally.

I have also discovered that it is easy once in power to be seduced away from keeping your eyes on the prize. It is so easy to become caught up and enamored with other things than the work at hand. You always have to know where you are, what results you're going for, and how to measure whether you're there.

You can't just be running around talking about being engaged; you have to actually be engaged. You can't just talk about others living up to their responsibilities; you have to be living up to yours as well. And if there is not a group following you, then you're not leading. If you're not leading, then you are not a leader. Trying to go it alone or trying to marginalize some groups so that you can expedite your own desires is just more of the same old politics.

THE YOUNG ELECTED OFFICIALS NETWORK

The Visionary

If the middle-school vending machines in Gainesville, Florida, had offered a certain brand of nacho cheese chips, there might not be a YEO (Young Elected Officials) Network. Seventh-grader Andrew Gillum, brand new to politics, circulated a petition as his first official act in office on the Student Council. "We had those tortilla-chip things that never had enough cheese on them," he explains years later. Unfortunately for him and his classmates, county nutrition rules banned the coveted nacho chips. "But," he says, "that was my first foray into understanding what it means to organize people around an idea

and a political movement—even if not successful."

Despite that early setback, Gillum (above) can count as a glowing success the growth of The Network, which he founded a dozen years later—not long after he became, at age twenty-three, the youngest person ever elected to the Tallahassee City Commission. He made his way there through politics at Florida A&M, serving as student-body president his senior year in a charged atmosphere, as Florida underwent a contentious and controversial mandatory voter recount that played a role in the 2000 election of President George W. Bush.

Jeb Bush, governor at the time, was the invited commencement speaker at A&M. Gillum announced to the media that he would lead graduating students and their families and friends in a public protest if Gov. Bush showed up. Gillum believed the governor had collaborated in "the botched election that propelled his brother to the presidency." Bush later sent regrets to the university president, citing a schedule conflict.

Gillum came away with a valuable lesson and a direction: "It really piqued my interest in politics and the social change movement from a totally different perspective—the idea that power doesn't listen; you have to *force* it to listen." He saw young people as an untapped national reserve of political energy, recognizing that if he wanted the perspective of young people represented in political circles, he would have to fight to effect that change.

His concerns were confirmed in his work after college as an organizer for People for the American Way. He traveled across the state of Florida, walking neighborhoods and knocking on doors, trying to register people to vote. Over and over, he faced discouragement as he encountered young people and others who didn't even know who their elected officials were. Severe hopelessness and an extreme lack of faith in the political system held the day, and these had led to widespread apathy.

When Gillum was elected to the Tallahassee City Commission in 2003, he was still learning the ropes of politics. He felt gratified and honored to hold elected office at an age much younger than most of those with whom he served, but there was one thing he didn't feel—accepted. Instead, other elected officials often made him feel like a kid playing a grown-ups' game—like a high school basketball player on an NBA team or a young guest at someone else's thirty-year high school reunion.

Just about everywhere he went in the course of his political life, he was referred to as "the new guy" or "the young guy." And he often felt that way himself. Whenever he went to a political convention or other event, he always seemed to be the only one asking where the restroom was or where he could find the coffee.

Gillum heard other elected officials say—sometimes to his face and sometimes behind his back—that they had shoes and socks older than he was, or something similar. "The insults seemed funny at the time," he reflects, "but they were demeaning to me."

While he felt like a fish out of water, he sensed that somewhere there might be—or at least *should* be—an ocean for himself and other young officials, even if he had to create and fill that ocean himself. Gillum knew that there had to be other young elected officials out there who felt as isolated and unsupported as he did. And he had a deep-seated need to find them.

At that time, he had no idea how many others like him there were in political office across the country. But he knew there were at least a few, because every now and then in the course of his activities on the political circuit, he had run into them. In fact he had some of their phone numbers. So Gillum took his cell phone out of his pocket and began calling every young elected official he could find. His message was, "What do you think of a few of us getting together to talk about forming a support group for young people in elected office?"

Gillum didn't know then that the simple act of dialing his phone would be the start of something so large and transformational. But he did understand that when it comes to real change in society, strength in numbers can be a very powerful force.

Soon, others were willing to help him carry the torch. One young official Gillum had come across was Alisha Thomas Morgan, who in November 2002 had become the first African American to serve Cobb County in the Georgia House of Representatives. When she started helping with logistics, "there was no stopping the momentum," says Gillum.

Seed money came from People for the American Way for a gathering of a dozen young leaders in Atlanta in the winter of 2004. Among the group at that initial strategy meeting were Kansas State Senator Katie Sieben, Texas State Representative Jacquin Castro, and his brother Juan Castro, the mayor of San Antonio. "There was an amazing spirit in the group," Gillum recalls, "and they all said we needed this."

A year later, sixty-four young elected officials met at the National Press Club in Washington, DC, to officially launch the YEO Network—more than twice as many as Gillum had dared to hope for. Today, the group that was at one time just a collection of names in Andrew Gillum's phone has grown to a nationwide network of more than six hundred young officeholders, and the number increases every year. An estimated 5 percent of elected officials across the country are under thirty-five, and nearly half of those are YEO Network members. Though the group is for those elected when younger than thirty-five, no member ever ages out, unless he or she chooses to do so.

The Network

The YEO Network is a nonpartisan, nonprofit organization that seeks to provide encouragement, training, resources, and emotional support for young elected officials across the country, who are attempting to advance in politics and improve their communities, based on the values of freedom, fairness, and opportunity. In addition to an annual convening, it provides mentor services, development seminars, scholarship programs, web events, workshops, and other training events—all aimed at helping young politicians increase their skill-sets and supplying the tools they need to transform their political vision into action. The Network is both a launching pad and a community of support and encouragement.

New members almost instantly feel relief when they discover that as successful, young politicians, they aren't alone in the world—even if, until finding the Network, they felt alone in their own little corner of it. When those who have been affected by the Network—or, more accurately, *touched* by it—are asked about their experience, often the most interesting and telling quality about their responses isn't what they say, but the glowing tone in which they say it.

Raquel Simon-Petley, the program manager for the YEO Network, says that from the very first day the group began organizing, there was a feeling that this was something really special. She still remembers very clearly the feelings she experienced when she attended the first convening of the group. The most striking thing, she says, was the intense camaraderie all the young leaders felt as soon as they got together in the same room with others who had similar goals, interests, and experiences.

There were issue- and skill-based sessions, ranging from effective messaging and coalition building to dealing positively with the media, and she remembers everyone furiously taking notes. "I was absolutely struck by how passionate and intelligent all these people in the room were," she says. "And they were all about my age. I was twenty-four at the time, and I was sitting next to a twenty-two-year-old mayor, who was in his last year because he was retiring from political office. That's when it hit me. I remember looking at him and asking myself: What am I doing with *my* life?"

The Network provides young leaders a vibrant platform for the exchange of ideas. It also connects them with policy development organizations and other political resources to help them transform their visions into progressive, political action on behalf of their communities, states, and the nation. But perhaps most important, they come together to be revitalized, to be baptized once again in the sea of energy and enthusiasm that arises spontaneously when likeminded people with a common cause and similar experiences come together.

The Network's three specific areas of focus—building a nationwide network, providing policy support and resources, and training members in the political skills necessary to effect change back home—are supported by specific programs.

The YEO Policy Academy convenes meetings on a variety of topics, such as redistricting, immigration reform, neighborhood stabilization, and foreclosure issues. The academies are formal weekend training events that bring together young elected officials for an intense and deep immersion in a specific policy issue, intended to enhance critical skills needed to deal with that issue, as well as teaching strategies for effective change.

Young People For is a long-term strategic initiative, supported through the People for the American Way Foundation. It was started in 2004 as a counterbalance to the radical Right's offering of resources and guidance to young ultraconservatives. It's an effort to increase the commitment, activism, and leadership of young progressives. Young People For attempts to promote progressive values among future leaders and to provide those leaders with opportunities to become strong advocates for social change in the communities where they live and serve.

The Front Line Leaders Academy (FLLA) helps to train the next generation of national leaders, providing them with a wide variety of skills ranging from community organizing to leadership development and campaigning skills. This intensive, eight-month program provides one-on-one support and makes use of campaign experts and other highly qualified instructors.

The Results

One very important thing the Young Elected Officials Network offers is an antidote to the natural intimidation and inferiority complex young leaders often experience. Megan England, who was elected in 2007 to the City Council of Roeland Park, Kansas, says YEO helped her grow her belief in herself. "The group shows people that effort and faith together can lead to great things—even when you're younger than everyone else in the game. Young people see others their age in leadership roles effecting change, and it creates a lasting impression. What we may lack in experience, we make up for in energy and enthusiasm."

Melvin Carter, a city councilman in St. Paul, Minnesota, says that before he got involved with the Network, he always felt like an outsider. He had always viewed politicians as "they," and when he got elected, he realized, "I am *they*. And if I say, They ought to fix this street, I'm talking about me." He encourages young people who are, "out to change the world for the better, to run and never let your age stop you. The person I want to vote for is someone who has volunteered in the schools or walked the picket line with the union or has taken their activism as far as they can and can then say they are called to further service."

Elesha Gayman, who served in the Iowa House of Representatives, says young people are a key to the vitality of any state. She wanted to take a political stand and fight, rather than leave the state, as so many others her age had. "I came to the point," she says, "where I was either going to be part of the problem and leave the state, or I was going to be part of the solution and change why young people are leaving—and work for opportunities here. Bringing that voice for change was what really propelled my campaign for our generation."

Gayman lives near the state border, where there is a billboard that she sees frequently: IOWA—FIELDS OF OPPORTUNITY. She wants to help others realize the opportunity. Her experience is that, "In our generation, if we are willing to put the time and effort into the community and areas we represent, residents are willing to give us opportunities to make that change we envision."

Henry Beck, who serves in Maine's House of Representatives, says the work YEO does is vitally important. All young elected officials, he says, need to understand how important an agent of change they can be for a group that often does not have a say in government. "Sometimes you are the only voice of the people you represent—don't forget it," Beck exhorts.

Bill Luton, who serves on the Elizabeth City/Pasquotank Board of Education in North Carolina, says that due to his youth he often finds himself going against the grain in the political world. Many people enter politics "and fight tooth and nail to preserve the status quo. But I got into the game for exactly the opposite reason—to shatter the status quo and make positive change. Young people bring something to the political game, an important quality of youth—a natural tendency to question the status quo." He hopes for a new era in which politicians don't see themselves as politicians but as "change agents."

Laketa Cole, a former city councilwoman from Cincinnati, Ohio, is an example of how a young politician can beat the odds, no matter how much the deck is stacked against her. "I had seven strikes against me when I decided to run for office," Cole says. "I'm young. I'm a woman. I'm black. I didn't have any money or name recognition. I didn't have a job. And I didn't have a major political party endorsement." None of that kept her from winning.

When she ran against twenty-seven other candidates in an at-large race, some of them were spending hundreds of thousands of dollars. Laketa developed the name "Cole Train" for her campaign. "I had these little train pins," she explains, "reminding people of the story of the engine that kept saying, 'I think I can, I think I can.' It worked, and I won."

Alisha Thomas Morgan says, "When you're a young elected official, you feel like you're an island. In many ways, you don't think anyone understands you. It seems that everyone has lessons they need to teach you, and you get treated like everyone's little niece or nephew. Sometimes you need to be reminded that what you bring to the table is valuable and that your age is not the qualifier. What matters is your experience, desire, and courage."

Antonio French, St. Louis alderman, says, "I travel between different worlds every day. I'm with gang members at night and hanging with the governor in the morning. I'm at a liquor store working to get the drug dealers off the front door, and an hour later I'm with multimillion-dollar developers. So much of our work is about bouncing around those different worlds, relating to these people, letting them know you are there and you really do care."

Lee May, county commissioner in DeKalb County, Georgia, remarks that all politics is local, and young elected officials learn quickly that "everyone wants something." Even those with the best of intentions want something. It's important to keep your eyes open and look more deeply into what is being asked of you, says May. "People will butter you up and tell you how great you are; then they'll make 'the big ask.' At that point, I have to brace myself and say, OK, alrighty—"

Sean Becker, mayor of Bozeman, Montana, believes a young elected official's best asset is an open mind. "We are not jaded. We don't owe people; we're not filled with political indebtedness or captive to a large network of political allegiances. Our ability to move freely and compete in the arena of ideas helps create new possibilities for our communities."

Every elected official has his or her own stories and lessons. Some elected leaders can be most effective by swinging to an extreme to frame and push their issues and agenda. The strategy is to fight for x, y, and z. Hopefully, you'll get z.

"When I fight for those issues, I want them all," says Becker. "My leadership style is consensus building and compromise and inviting the opposition to the table. Usually, I find they all want similar outcomes, even if we disagree on the process to get to those outcomes."

Nevada Littlewolf, city councilor in Virginia, Minnesota, agrees with Mayor Becker's style, but she says it is not always easy and takes a personal toll, especially on a young elected official. One of her advisors told her that she needed to grow a thicker skin. "I asked her if there is a particular, special lotion I can buy to give me that kind of skin!"

Jesse Mermell, selectman of the town of Brookline, Massachusetts, recognizes that there are no guarantees of winning as a young candidate, but the fear of losing should not keep young people from getting involved. "Don't wait, and don't be afraid to lose," she advises. "If you lose, lose well. By running a good, respectable campaign, people can learn about you, and in turn you can learn about your community. It can be such an asset to you personally, for your own goals and to your political future. The most important thing I did after I lost was go to my opponents' election-night parties and shake their hands and talk to their supporters. I only stopped by for fifteen minutes each, but that made a huge difference for people coming around to supporting me the next year. If you run a good race that you're proud of, there is nothing to lose."

Jay Chen, president of California's Hacienda-La Puente School Board, says that, in the 21st century, leadership by young people doesn't end at the borders of their communities: "What we do in America impacts everyone around us, whether through domestic or foreign policy. Young people need to take the opportunity to go out and explore, to be prepared to lead in a more interconnected and diverse world."

Progressive young leaders want change. Steve Wukela beat the incumbent by one vote to become mayor of Florence, South Carolina, in 2008. "Nothing is more unlikely of success or more hazardous to its proponent than change," says Wukela. "I remember reading Machiavelli's *The Prince*. He wrote that change is hard to a fault and tough to bring to fruition. As a candidate with a platform of change, I find that to be a reasonable statement. I'm sure President Obama can identify with that statement, too."

The Reason

Brooklyn, New York, Democratic Committeeman Samuel Pierre is working the shiny black piano. With a crowd of young elected officials surrounding him, he feels like he's Duke Ellington, and the joyous crowd singing along is his orchestra. We're in the Crystal City Sheraton at the edge of Washington, DC, and we've been here for about an hour. The sun is barely peeking through the windows, and with each new breath we find ourselves more fully in the moment.

Milwaukee County Supervisor Marina Dimitrijevic's voice switches from melody to a sweet hum, as this group of twenty or so clusters together with arms around one another, swaying and clapping as we finish up another Motown tune. Shouts of joy and Amen! fill the air. The spirit is freewheeling, and the celebration is showing no signs whatsoever of dying down.

Melvin Carter, the St. Paul city councilman, flashes a smile as Andrew Gillum approaches. Melvin whispers a number like a divine message to Samuel Pierre, with an affirming nod and a pat on his back. The bass keys start, and immediately the music grabs our full attention. Collectively, we nod and smile and move to the rhythm. The sound is familiar, and our hearts and minds feel as if in full alignment.

Others gather, drawn like bees to honey. Karen Liot Hill, city councilor of Lebanon, New Hampshire, and Megan England, Roeland

Park, Kansas, councilor start swaying. Pasadena, California, City Councilor Jacque Robinson makes the circle complete. South Bend City Councilman Henry Davis flexes his shoulders as his hand slides over his goatee. Andrew Gillum rolls up his shirtsleeves, and an air of inevitably takes over.

The emotion builds in a crescendo of camaraderie and joy—and the freedom that comes from a spirit of mutual identification and admiration. We feel a common bond wrap us more tightly together in service to a vision greater than ourselves. The song has become a symbol and theme song for the YEO Network. And it has also become a great source of affirmation and strength.

> Sometimes in our lives, we all have pain, we all have sorrow.
> But if we are wise, we know that there's always tomorrow.
>
> Lean on me, when you're not strong,
> And I'll be your friend,
> I'll help you carry on.
> For, it won't be long,
> 'Til I'm gonna need
> Somebody to lean on.
>
> OH, IT WON'T BE LO-O-ONG,
> 'TIL I'M GONNA NEED SOMEBODY TO LE-E-EAN ON.

The chorus swells and drives the simple but vital message home.

> So just call on me, brother, when you need a hand.
> We all need
> WE ALL NEED SOMEBODY TO LE-E-E-EAN ON.
> I just might have a problem that you'd understand.
> WE ALL NEED SOMEBODY TO LE-E-E-EAN ON.

As my colleagues and I sang the last line of "Lean on Me" at the fifth Convening of the Young Elected Officials Network, we knew we weren't just singing about the work we had before us: the talking points, position statements, and news cycles to attend to. The message was clear, and we felt it filling the air in the music all around us: We not only can, but we must lean on one another, if we are to win a future grounded in traditional wisdom. Through our shared effort and responsibility, we can create a renewed and vibrant America, in gratitude for those who've pioneered before us and in hope for generations to come.

We know this, because young leaders of every generation have answered the call to be *On Point*—to dedicate their lives and leadership during times of great challenge and uncertainty toward the perpetual becoming of a great nation.

PROFILE UPDATES

Anton J. Gunn

Anton was appointed Regional Director at the U.S. Department of Health and Human Services (Region IV) by President Obama in 2010. His responsibilities included implementing the new Health Care Reform Law. Most recently, Anton was appointed the director of the Office of External Affairs, focused on making Health and Human Services more inclusive, transparent, and accountable. On Valentine's Day 2012, Anton visited Arlington National Cemetery with his brother to celebrate what would have been Cheron's 34th birthday. Anton loves spending time with his young daughter, Ashley, and one day they will undoubtedly dance to the greatest father-daughter wedding medley ever.

Faith Winter

Faith became the first city councilor in Westminster to have children while serving. She now has a three-year-old and a one-year-old. Both children have become "community babies" and enjoy going to town halls, ribbon cuttings, and hearings. One of Faith's proudest accomplishments was saving Westminster's domestic violence program. During tough budget decisions in 2010, the city—which can process a domestic violence claim in forty-eight hours on average—was on the verge of delegating the program to the county, which can take from two to six weeks to process a claim, lowering conviction rates and increasing repeat incidents. Faith led the charge to save the program and has worked to protect the most vulnerable citizens in Westminster. She was reelected to a second term in 2011, and was subsequently elected by her colleagues as mayor pro tem.

Alex Cornell du Houx

Alex received a direct commission from the Navy as a public affairs officer; he conducts operational support for U.S. Central Command (Middle East operations).

During this legislative session of 2012, he defended Maine's renewable-energy portfolio, which has boosted the state's economy, according to a recent London Economics report. He successfully created a law to weatherize the Statehouse, as he believes we should lead by example and save taxpayer money. Alex passed legislation to reduce the state's dependency on oil, which has been used as model legislation in other states. He also wrote legislation praised by Gov. LePage, to protect oil and gas consumers.

Alex is working with the Inaugural Young Leaders Climate Action Network program, which brings elected officials and future leaders from across the nation together to combat climate change.

Currently, he is leading a State Department sponsored trip to Australia to foster government-to-government relations. This is the first-ever delegation of veterans who are elected officials and work in government to participate in the program. They meet with members of parliament, administration, and NGOs for two weeks. Australian delegates will then come to the United States to do the same. It is run through the American Council of Young Political Leaders. Alex has conducted similar trips to Indonesia and Malaysia.

Alisha Thomas Morgan

Alisha was elected to her fifth term in office and finished writing a book, *No Apologies: Powerful Lessons in Life, Love, and Politics*. She has been named one of fifteen Next Generation African American Women under 40 to Know in Politics in America by The Political Girl. Alisha continues to be a pioneering figure in the Young Elected Officials Network and the Georgia Legislature.

Matt Heinz

Matt won reelection to the Arizona State House in 2010, during one of the worst political moments in history for Democrats in the state. Despite the supermajority status of the Republicans in the Legislature, he has shepherded more than a dozen measures through the political process, then across the governor's desk and into law. In January 2012, Matt announced his first run for the U.S. House of Representatives. If successful, he will fill the seat previously held by Rep. Gabrielle Giffords, who resigned following the January 2011 shooting in Tucson, during which she was severely injured. In addition to his legislative duties, Matt continues to practice medicine at the Tucson Medical Center.

Dominic Frongillo

Dominic wrote from a rural village in KwaZulu-Natal, South Africa, with an update on the UN climate negotiations. He expressed his concerns regarding hydraulic fracturing and the future of the Kyoto Protocol. During his South Africa trip, Dominic had a "brief but awesome" chat with musician Dave Matthews in Johannesburg.

Rashida H. Tlaib

Rashida was among ten citizens nationwide honored on the inaugural Heroes list by Immigrants' List, a bipartisan political action committee. She was also named Citizen of the Year by the Wayne State University School of Social Work Alumni Association. She now has a baby boy, Yousif, whose older brother, Adam, is turning seven. Rashida and her husband, Fayez, are celebrating fourteen years of marriage.

Rodney Glassman

Rodney completed his term on the Tucson City Council, and his family has moved north to Phoenix. He is now the director of Public Sector Solutions for Waste Management Arizona/New Mexico. He's currently serving as a captain in the U.S. Air Force JAG Reserve Corps and will be attending Squadron Officer School at Maxwell Air Force Base in Montgomery, Alabama. Rodney serves on the Executive Board of the Grand Canyon Boy Scouts of America, the nation's fifth largest Boy Scout council. Most important, since our interview, Rodney and his wife, Sasha, have welcomed a "beautiful, smart, and wonderful daughter."

Janet Chin

Janet was reelected in November 2011 to the Garvey School Board and is now the communications director for California State Senator Dr. Ed

Hernandez. The M. Janet Chin Youth Foundation is celebrating its fifth anniversary, and its programs are going strong, creating jobs for youth and transitional adults. The school district has a new, highly qualified superintendent, who is moving forward to ensure students are skilled for 21st century jobs and citizenry. Janet and her husband live in the city of Rosemead, where she grew up and is raising her three sons, Keno, Korbin, and Kasden.

Simeon Queen

Simeon created PastorSimQ.com and "It's taking off with sermon-songs like 'The Amazing.'" He has created a line of popular Jesus Swag T-shirts and finished his book, *The Church or the Club—Who's Winning?* Simeon still faithfully serves homeless people through St. John's Downtown United Methodist Church in Houston and attributes all that he has done and will do to simply being obedient to the will of God.

Marisol Cruz

Marisol is now serving as president of the Lennox United School System. She is increasing community ownership and seeking out new leadership roles for others in the school district through the creation of an Arts and Culture Committee. Marisol continues to balance her leadership with her responsibilities as a single mother parenting two pre-teen sons, Samuel Wayne and Ishmael, as they become young men.

Sara Humm

Sara's four-year term as an Ottawa City Commissioner expired in April 2011. She was proud to serve and was appointed mayor pro tem for two of those years. When her elected term was ending, she served as the campaign manager for a successful local campaign and loved every minute of it. In May 2011, Sara received her bachelor's degree from Ottawa University in Ottawa, Kansas, with distinction in her major: communications, with concentrations in journalism and public relations. During her senior year, Sara was elected student body president and was a proud staff member of the award-winning student newspaper, *The*

Campus, as the photography editor. She is currently in graduate school, pursuing her passion for photography on the side.

Kevin Killer

After finishing the legislative session in South Dakota, Kevin filed to run for reelection. He has helped start a nonprofit on the Pine Ridge Reservation, named the Native Youth Leadership Alliance (NYLA). NYLA embraces indigenous approaches to leadership and community building for students at tribal colleges. Kevin is hoping to carve out more time for himself and maybe play some basketball.

Shane Cohn

Shane started a small-scale urban farming initiative, when he bought two chicks named Elizabeth and Frieda. He built a coop and chicken area in his backyard and faithfully collects an eco-friendly and sustainable supply of eggs each day. Shane is working on a citywide bike-sharing program, LGBT initiatives, and a couple of redevelopment projects, and is still trying to reform city government. When he's not working on reelecting President Obama, he is training for a half-marathon, doing a whole bunch of yoga, and starting to think about reelection.

Kyrsten Sinema

Kyrsten resigned her state Senate seat in early 2012 to run for an open seat for U.S. Congress in Arizona's District 9. When she is not out knocking on doors and accumulating endorsements, she is teaching in the School of Social Work at the Arizona State University downtown campus or in the School of Justice and Social Inquiry at the ASU Tempe campus.

She is a regular on local news and talk shows in Phoenix, has made several appearances on *The Keith Olbermann Show*, and is working on a follow-up to her first book, *Unite and Conquer.*

Kyrsten has completed a number of marathons over the past six months and will be running in a crowded and competitive Democratic primary. During her down time, she enjoys an occasional hike to a gorgeous Arizona sunrise.

Airick Leonard West

Airick has led the Kansas City United School District as chair through difficult times over the past two years. He has successfully sought aggressive reforms to address the financial difficulties with the school system and the cultural/institutional realities that hold back achievement, particularly in the areas of early learning and community engagement.

Airick is the state treasurer of the Missouri Democratic Party and currently recruiting and training potential candidates through the School Board School. He kept his pledge to serve only one term, which will end in December 2012. After a strong lobbying effort by citizens to reconsider his decision not to run for a second term, Airick filed as a write-in candidate for reelection at the last minute and won easily. He was then immediately sworn in and elected board president once again.

ACKNOWLEDGMENTS

When I started this project, I had no idea where things were going, but I seemed to make good time. I originally wanted to interview a variety of young elected officials across the political spectrum—progressive and conservative, right and left—and see how things developed. Dr. Ruth Mandel and Rutgers University's Eagleton Institute of Politics offered good advice as I started down this road. The Institute's groundbreaking work on the Young Elected Leaders Project offered great source information. My friend and former Guilford College professor Dr. Bill Schmickle thought a book that focused on the stories and motivations behind young political leaders was a great idea. In addition to being a great teacher, Bill wrote the most politically stimulating (and only) book on historic preservation I've ever read.

Thanks to Raquel Simon and Ryan Hurst for all the logistical support on my way to the Young Elected Officials (YEO) Convening in Atlanta in June 2010. Conversations that stoked the creative fires came from: Jeremiah Grace, Yiaway Yeh, Carl Sciortino, Tim Geimel, Quentilla Cato, Megan England, Karim Camera, Darrell Gaston, Cara Jennings, Jason Overman, Ezra Temko, Tony Mandrigal, Paul Roales, Nevada Littlewolf, Alan B. Williams, Sean Garballey, Carmelo Garcia, Trinity Donovan, Dave Woodard, Carl M. Sciortino, Jr., Anders Ibsen, Brandan Buchanan, Karen Liot Hill, Jeremy VanMeter, Angela Garretson, Michael Maturo, Paul Roales, Nathan Shinagawa, Henry Davis, Jr., and Zach Foutch. And thanks to Janet Chin and Kyrsten Sinema for taking my young daughter, Elle, under their wings. She felt like the most beautiful girl in the world as she sported her new pair of glasses ("Sinemas") at the YEO Convening in 2011.

I want to thank a number of young conservatives I met along the way, with great stories and insights into politics and public service. Milan, Michigan, Mayor Pro Tem Michael Armitage; Waterville, Ohio, Mayor Derrick Merrin; Ryan Bingham, mayor of Torrington, Connecticut; and former Newark, Ohio, Councilor Cherri Hottinger were all a pleasure to get to know. I enjoyed talking to Lenior, North Carolina, City Councilor T. J. Rhor, a great Libertarian voice. Their stories were not profiled because of my ultimate decision to focus *On Point* on young, center-to-left progressives, but their service to their communities is to be commended and appreciated.

The running joke about progressive leaders is that they can't figure out what they believe in, much less give that message consistently to voters. The young messengers profiled here burst that stereotype with their passion, clarity, and courage. In a time of unprecedented partisanship and "disconnect" on almost every level of government, *On Point* relates the stories of young people rooted in their own fervently held hopes, dreams, and aspirations—while attempting to avoid the rancor and partisanship that are rife in political discourse these days. My hope is that what is fundamentally American will emerge throughout the book.

I want to thank the one hundred young elected officials I have interviewed. *On Point* profiles sixteen of these leaders. That means there are a number of stories that are not told here, but they are nonetheless incredibly unique. Lorraine Ahern lent her ears on occasion and helped brainstorm ideas on what to do with all these great stories.

To the young leaders profiled, you were very generous with your time in sharing your stories, the experiences that shaped your leadership styles, and the advice to other young people who might consider running for public office. I cannot express my appreciation enough to you for becoming partners in this project, and I feel confident that your stories will be read for years to come.

I want to thank Polar Bear and Company, particularly Paul and Ramona Cornell du Houx, for publishing *On Point*. They enthusiastically bought into the book's concept and were encouraging all along the way.

Senator George J. Mitchell's contribution of the foreword is a great honor. I spent time with Senator Mitchell during his visit to Guilford College several years ago and have always appreciated his principled leadership and skill in negotiation and peacemaking. My special thanks to Rep. Alex Cornell du Houx, a former Mitchell Scholar, for his help with Senator Mitchell's office and helping put it all together.

A special thanks to Attorneys Lynn Szymoniak and O. Max Gardner III. Lynn is a homeowner who was featured on CBS's *60 Minutes* in 2011 for uncovering details about banks' robo-signing of foreclosure documents. Max is the best bankruptcy defense attorney I know. Both have an unparalleled commitment to justice and basic fairness for the people most impacted by our recent financial crisis. They've been there for me on countless occasions in my role as register of deeds, and their integrity and service set the bar high for future leaders.

A number of family, friends, and colleagues have to be mentioned. Without them I would not have written this book. Geraldine and the late Thomas H. Thigpen, Julie and Anthony Brown, Michael Thigpen,

Dion Currie, Laura Seel, John Parker, Jason Smith, Z Holler, Jim Peavy, Sue Stuckey, Carole Simpson, Bob Landreth, Melvin "Skip" Alston, and Cheryl Wilson. Dr. James Calabro was my chief medical advisor on this project.

As always, our families can be a great source of strength, support, and good humor. My wife, Michelle, juggled her schedule to help me complete interviews and attend YEO Convenings. She's now ready to unleash my talents on a litany of projects around the house. Our children, Elle and Aiden, think it's cool that their dad is an author, but really want to use the computer now. Thanks to Denny Coughlin and the extended family in Johnson City, New York.

I want to thank my old friend Rev. Z Holler, who suggested Joyce Hollyday as an editor. For that, Z has my eternal thanks. Joyce was my editor, but her job description expanded quickly to sounding board, active listener, counselor, and friend. And the last couple of years have not been easy. Her mother passed from this life after a long bout with Alzheimer's. It is a disease that raises every issue—moral, spiritual, philosophical, and political. Joyce handled them all thoughtfully, with passion and with grace. And it's a testimony to her skill in a book of first-person narratives that I consistently heard the word "Cool!" after participants reviewed her edited drafts.

In conclusion, I'd like to thank the people Guilford County, North Carolina, who have given me their vote and the opportunity to serve them over the past fourteen years.

Jeff Thigpen grew up in a small farming community in southeastern North Carolina. At age twenty-seven, he was elected the youngest county commissioner in North Carolina and the youngest ever in Guilford County. He has served with distinction in elected office for fourteen years and is currently the Guilford County register of deeds. As in his writing, the author demonstrates that strong leadership in the 21st century needs boldness and courage, good humor, and pragmatism to leave our neighborhoods better than we found them.

Jeff received a BA in political science, and in justice & policy studies from Guilford College and an MA in public affairs from the University of North Carolina at Greensboro, and he is a graduate of the North Carolina Institute of Political Leadership. He has received several awards, including the Tyre Tyler Outstanding Young Democrat in North Carolina, the Martin Luther King, Jr. Award from UNC-Greensboro, and the North Carolina Association of County Commissioner's (NCACC) Local Government Federal Credit Union Productivity award for creating efficiencies in county government. He is also a member of the Young Elected Officials Network.

He lives in Greensboro with his wife, Michelle, an elementary school principal, and their two children, Elle (8) and Aiden (4).